TEN GROWING
SOVIET CHURCHES

TEN GROWING
SOVIET CHURCHES

by
Lorna and Michael Bourdeaux

MARC EUROPE
Keston College Book No 17
(The Moorhouse Lectures, Australia)

British Library Cataloguing in Publication Data

Bourdeaux, Lorna
    Ten growing Soviet Churches.
    1. Church growth—Soviet Union
    I. Title   II. Bourdeaux, Michael
    274.7'0828   BR936

    ISBN 0–947697–47–0 (MARC)
          0–905870-01–8 (Keston)

Unless otherwise noted, Scripture quotations in this publication are from the Holy Bible, New International Version, Copyright © 1973, 1978, 1984, International Bible Society. Published by Hodder and Stoughton. Used by permission.

MARC Europe is an integral part of World Vision, an international Christian humanitarian organisation. MARC's object is to assist Christian leaders with factual information surveys, management skills, strategic planning and other tools for evangelism. MARC Europe also publishes and distributes related books on matters of mission, church growth, management, spiritual maturity and other topics.

Keston College is a research and information centre, monitoring the situation for religious believers of all faiths in the countries of Eastern Europe and the Soviet Union.

To Adrian Francis
whose imminence caused the joint authorship
of this book

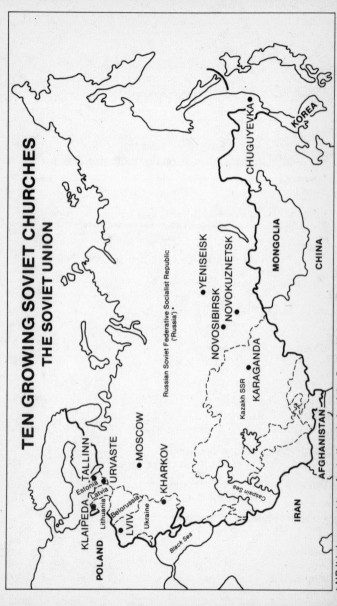

TEN GROWING SOVIET CHURCHES
THE SOVIET UNION

KLAIPEDA
TALLINN
URVASTE
POLAND
Estonia
Latvia
Lithuania
Belorussia
LVIV
Ukraine
MOSCOW
KHARKOV
Black Sea
Caspian Sea

Russian Soviet Federative Socialist Republic
('Russia') *

YENISEISK
NOVOSIBIRSK
NOVOKUZNETSK
Kazakh SSR
KARAGANDA

CHUGUYEVKA
KOREA
MONGOLIA
CHINA

IRAN
AFGHANISTAN

* NB It is incorrect to refer to the whole of the Soviet Union as 'Russia'.

CONTENTS

THE MOORHOUSE LECTURES

The Moorhouse Lectures have been delivered in Melbourne since 1907. The lectureship was established to honour the leadership and inspiration of the Reverend James Moorhouse DD who was Bishop of Melbourne 1876–1886. In 1905 a minute of St Paul's Cathedral Chapter defined the subject of the lectures as:

— the defence and confirmation of the Christian faith as declared in the Apostle's and Nicene creeds;

— questions bearing upon the history and authority of the Holy Scriptures of the Old and New Testaments;

— the social aspects of the Christian faith in their widest application.

Since that time there have been 38 lectures offering a remarkably diverse range of topics. Amongst these more recent contributors have been Bryan Green, Stephen Neill, Douglas Webster, David Jenkins, CFD Moule, Marcus Loane and Ronald Preston.

I am delighted that the Founder and General Director of Keston College, the Reverend Michael Bourdeaux, has accepted my invitation to present this material in Melbourne at the 1987 Moorhouse Lectures. Through Keston College, Michael and Lorna Bourdeaux have made a significant contribution to our understanding of the Churches in Eastern Europe. This important study, *Ten Growing Soviet Churches*, will widen that influence even further.

David Penman
Archbishop of Melbourne

FOREWORD

The genesis of this book was rather unusual. The publishers originally approached Lorna, my wife, to write it after they had seen her first book, *Barinov: The Trumpet Call*, a biography of the Leningrad Christian rock musician, Valeri Barinov. She agreed, but with reservations about a deadline, because she was in the early days of her first pregnancy. However, she quickly became deeply involved and produced five chapters. After all, the challenge was exciting: to show the world that it was possible to write a book on ten growing Soviet churches. It led her to explore some churches in the Soviet Union which do not normally receive much publicity.

Then a new factor appeared in the reckoning. Just as Lorna was beginning to fear that the increasing obligations to future family were making it impossible to foresee when she could finish the book, I decided that the text of the Moorhouse Lectures which I was preparing was not quite right for the occasion. This is a series which takes place every other year in Melbourne, Australia, and I was honoured to be selected as the speaker for 1987. Suddenly I realised that what my wife was writing was far more suitable than my work for a series of lectures to a public for many of whom the subject of the Church under Communism would be a new one.

Archbishop David Penman of Melbourne and his Moorhouse committee were most accommodating and agreed to the change, so I took over the text and wrote the last five chapters. In all this, the British publishers have been both flexible and accommodating. In their turn they are grateful to the Moorhouse committee for certain financial assistance which has made it possible to ensure that the published book will be available in Australia at the right time.

The final sequence we have chosen for the chapters intermingles our contributions. We felt it right, as each has contributed advice to the other, not to sign our individual work.

Keston College staff, too numerous to mention, have contributed their expertise to every chapter, but we must single out our typists, Mavis Perris, Lorna Forrester and Caroline Andrews, for special thanks.

Keston College, still unique in the English-speaking world as a centre for study of religion under Communism, has now burgeoned into an institution which is far larger and which plays much more of a public role than I ever imagined possible when a small group of us founded it in 1969. Its archive is perhaps the unsung hero of this book; in searching through its abundant riches for every chapter, we have been privileged to increase our own knowledge and to see even more clearly that human legislation and politics hostile to religion can never confine God's plan for the Christianisation of the world.

Michael Bourdeaux
Keston, Kent

INTRODUCTION

This is a book which, according to human canons, should never have been written. One of the main planks of the Bolshevik ideological and practical platform, as constructed by Lenin at the time of the Russian Revolution of October 1917, was that religion should die out. Karl Marx had predicted that the ideal society would have no place for it and it would wither away. Lenin, Stalin, Khrushchev and their successors all—in their individual ways—lent a helping hand to its demise.

And yet here we are, almost 70 years after the Revolution, with an embarrassment of riches from among which to select the evidence that there really are *Ten Growing Soviet Churches*. Furthermore, they are found within all the major historic divisions of Christianity: Catholic, Orthodox and Protestant. No major denomination in the Soviet Union had to be excluded because it was not exhibiting traits of growth. Two of Christendom's most ancient churches, the Armenian Apostolic and the Georgian Orthodox, are not included, but this is more because of lack of information in the present state of our knowledge rather than any conviction we have that they are static.

That there is a Protestant revival in the Soviet Union is relatively well known. However, it may well come as a surprise to many that this encompasses Baptists registered and unregistered (split into two churches), Pentecostals, Mennonites, Methodists and even Lutherans (the last for long considered the most quiescent of the major denominations of the Soviet Union).

To these we add Catholics, both Roman (official and registered) and of the Eastern Rite in Ukraine (banned by law). Revival here has been spurred on by, but not originally activated by, the election of a Polish Pope in 1978. No such 'divine intervention' from the outside explains the spontaneous revival in the Orthodox Church, which gives weight to the latter part of the book and the occurrence of which is still a tight-closed secret to the majority of Christians worldwide.

Nevertheless, the reader unfamiliar with the subject must be prepared to throw away many of the visible and statistical criteria by which he will judge Christian revival in other parts of the world. If we were to measure renewal by the development of Christian institutions, the erection of splendid church buildings and offices for staff and membership records, the establishment of publishing programmes or the introduction of imaginative educational projects for the young—then there would be no book. Therefore the reader is asked to set aside any preconceptions he may have from acquaintance with the church in Britain, the United States, Western Europe, Australasia, even the poorest parts of Latin America, Africa, India or other parts of Asia. Even with the Muslim world, where restrictions on evangelism are so stifling, the comparisons are so remote as to be barely worth making. Further, all Communist countries have restrictions on religion which originate from the same set of ideological preconceptions, but the practical application of these—from annihilation (Albania) to relative liberty (East Germany)—is so vastly different from country to country that comparisons are complicated, and we cannot entertain them here. These ten chapters refer to conditions which prevail in the Soviet Union alone.

It is instructive, therefore, to pause for a few moments to consider some of the factors which make it necessary to drop any preconceptions that originate from a knowledge of Christian revival elsewhere, and to run through them in a rather impressionistic way, leaving aside considerations of history, statistics, legislation and the practice of atheism—about which whole books have been written and on which some information will be found in tabulated form in the Appendix.

As we chose our ten examples, we kept certain criteria constantly in mind. Thirty years ago there was not enough information to hand to write a book of any sort about the current state of the churches in the Soviet Union (the first post-war book on the subject, *Religion in the Soviet Union*, by Walter Kolarz, was not published until 1961). Twenty years ago and another period of persecution later (under Khrushchev) the feeble evidence of religious revival was beginning to filter through, and this originated mostly from the Baptists. Ten years ago there was already a full flood of information, affecting Orthodox and Catholic churches alike.

Yet the information which now bulges out of the Keston College archive is different in kind, much of it, from what is available in other places about other parts of the world. Not much fact-finding can be done on the spot. Visa questions, travel restrictions on all foreign visitors and language difficulties see to this. One is confined to what Soviet citizens themselves gather, and only a small proportion of this is written up and evades the restrictions on the free flow of information. Therefore the data are very rarely systematic. A list of religious prisoners may be as complete, within the denomination, as the compilers can make it, but a preacher only too rarely furnishes us with the text of one of his sermons and he will, with good reason, keep the nature of his work with young people as closely guarded a secret as possible.

Not only do we have no access to church records, but

there are none, at least in the sense in which we understand them. The nearest equivalents lie in the archives of the government's Council on Religious Affairs, a body closely associated with the secret police, and no believer, give or take an occasional leaked document, has ever had access to them. Church authorities in Moscow will not even say categorically how many buildings they have open in their own capital city. The first count was done by a Western student (one of the authors) on foot.

The statistics held by the Council on Religious Affairs refer to registered—and therefore legal—churches. They will try to gather intelligence about illegal groups, but the latter will inevitably conceal as much as they can, sometimes even their very existence, from the prying eyes of the hostile state. There are no 'parishes' in the geographical sense, only registered and unregistered churches, the former especially having congregations swollen or decreased week by week by climatic and local travel conditions, or even by the control of the local police. (When we use the word 'parish' in this book, we mean the church and the people who go to it.) Into this sea of unclarity, one has to pour various currents of statistics which both government and church officials may have modified in response to all kinds of pressures and ideological considerations under which they operate. Only grass-roots opinion is entirely reliable, but contact with this is sporadic, leaving huge tracts of Soviet territory with which there is little or no contact.

Some of the ten churches are located in what is recognisably occupied territory—Estonian Methodists and Lutherans, Lithuanian Catholics—and the anti-imperialist feelings of the people must necessarily colour the life of the churches there. One whole denomination, the Pentecostals, used, until very recently, to be banned from having any independent existence. The group in Chuguyevka which we describe is still unregistered, as are the Baptists in Kharkov (Ukraine). In the Western Ukraine the major denomination of the people, the Eastern-Rite Catholic Church, was peremptorily abolished by the Soviets in 1946, yet it has persisted as an underground organisation in an amazing way. It was impossible to identify one specific 'congregation' about which we could write, but we did not feel therefore right to penalise these amazing people by omission.

Lest anyone should think that religious revival is a feature primarily in the context of colonialist oppression, we should point out its prevalence in the Orthodox Church, where the examples come from both Siberia and the capital city. Indeed, Moscow features also in the chapter on its registered Baptist church, disproving the contention of Soviet atheism that religious 'survival' (the word 'revival' could never be admitted) is a phenomenon of the culturally backward and the uneducated (the countryside) and of the old.

In setting aside all the standard criteria for appraising the life of a 'growing' church, one notes the absence of just about every advantage which Christians enjoy in most first-world and to a growing extent some third-world countries. To put it starkly, countless Africans worship in tin huts, but if they are literate they have access to Christian literature which speaks to their own condition in a wealth which is unimaginable to their Soviet counterparts (who may not even have the tin hut to worship in: see the account of the temporary tabernacle in Kharkov on pp 123).

Soviet Christians have no Christian literature in the sense in which we understand it. There is a most severe shortage of Bibles, prayer books and hymn books; concordances, commentaries, popular theology, church newspapers, song books for the young, teaching materials for children are banned by law or practice. Only a few scattered unofficial imports and *samizdat* (self-produced publications) provide an occasional oasis in the desert. Even registered churches lack the facilities which are standard in many other places: offices, meeting rooms, storage space and the most rudimentary toilets. The churches themselves are almost invariably too small for the demands made upon them. For decades we have had access to slide and film projectors and sound systems to help the audibility of preachers; now we are fast moving into the era of video equipment for teaching and micro-computers for record keeping. For a Soviet congregation, even a typewriter is a luxury (Fr Dimitri Dudko's was confiscated in a raid on his parish (see p. 194), and a typed information sheet is virtually unknown. While musical instruments are now sometimes permitted in churches to support congregational or choral singing (where the tradition of the denomination encourages this), to obtain instruments of satisfactory quality is just about impossible, unless one has foreign contacts. The poor quality of radio, tapes and tape-recordings inhibits making full use of foreign Christian broadcasts, although it does not prevent a ceaseless quest to exploit such possibilities to the full (see the cover photograph). Members of a collective farm may well band together to hire a lorry to drive to a distant church, but it would be unthinkable for a church to own its own minibus to aid fellowship outings or similar activities, which are, in any event, strictly against the law.

Much of what we take for granted is impossible legally or for practical reasons: evangelisation in all its many forms, teaching the faith to children, systematic parish visiting, charitable and social work, whether in hospitals, relief of the needy (especially the deprived families of Christian prisoners who receive no social security) or even making a casual donation to Oxfam—because there is no Soviet equivalent. There is no vehicle for a Soviet Christian to express his view to the public at large, the air waves and the pages of the newspapers being closed to him if he expresses a Christian viewpoint.

Not all the clergy can be trained. The Russian Orthodox Church has three seminaries, but access to them is controlled by the state and the requisite residence permit will be granted only after it has approved of the candidate. The

one Catholic seminary in Lithuania is never permitted to
receive a Ukrainian or a Siberian. Methodists, Baptists,
Mennonites, Lutherans have no proper seminary at all.
Some fortunate students will have access to a correspondence course (without a back-up library), but many will be
denied even this all their preaching lives. That small proportion of people who respond to the call to full-time Christian ministry, and overcome all the obstacles, often find
themselves moved hither and thither at the whim of the
local representatives of the Council on Religious Affairs.
To build up a pastoral relationship with people over a long
period may therefore, in many instances, be impossible.

Nor are these restrictions always passive. The young, the
educated, and the managerial class will almost certainly encounter positive discrimination if their practice of the faith
becomes known; this will bar them from higher education
(and therefore from many professions), and from rising to
positions of responsibility if they slip through the net in the
first place. Believers often find themselves relegated to the
bottom of the housing list. The most active ('fanatical', in
Soviet terminology) will attract hostile articles in the Soviet
press, without right of reply, which may exacerbate the
feelings of neighbours against them. A Soviet court may decree the removal of children from such families (the law on
'Deprivation of Parental Rights', which enjoins the whole
population to bring up children in the 'spirit of the builder
of Communism', i.e. Lenin). In the most extreme cases (except that implementation of the law is unpredictable, with
some suffering for what others are able to do with relative
impunity) court cases lead to fines and then imprisonment.
For over 20 years Christian prisoners have consistently
been numbered in the hundreds and under Khrushchev in
the early 1960s it was in the thousands.

Yet the miracle has occurred, as St Paul said it would.
One of the world's poorest churches has succeeded in making many rich (II Cor. 6:10). The ten chapters which follow
illustrate the reality of the apostle's confident forecast:

countless Christians who have nothing yet possess everything that is spiritually worthwhile.

We may seek to define the sources of this growth: disillusionment with Marxist and materialist dogma, the example of outstanding evangelists, many of whom have illustrated a capacity to suffer which reflects the spirit of the Early Church in its fullness, the simple determination of the grandmother who teaches a few simple truths to the child on her knee, the high moral standards and hard work of a Christian family (as contrasted with the lack of these qualities in society at large), foreign radio broadcasts. We can even judge—rightly—that every available page of Christian literature is read more intently by dozens more people and valued a hundred times more highly than any of the superabundance of books available in other countries. But the final balance sheet is still so wildly wrong in human terms that no natural agency can explain the phenomenon of what has occurred in the Soviet Union over the last two decades.

The pages which follow are the fruits of painstaking research at Keston College which has gone on over a quarter of a century. They stick strictly to the realm of provable fact and do not invoke the miraculous. Yet, when the last full stop is written, something, we feel, has been encompassed which no academic compilation and assessment of sources can explain. Christ, for our generation, is most potently present in the suffering Church which he himself founded on Calvary. The Resurrection which followed is something which human analysis can never explain, but which countless Christians experience as reality. This book, we pray, will make more available to one part of God's creation the reality experienced by another. In return, we shall more readily share the spiritual riches of other kinds which we enjoy with those who, by circumstances of birth and upbringing, are denied them.

Chapter 1

Estonian Methodists: Music and Ministry

The Kremlin is registering the shock wave of Christian revival on its seismograph. No tremor on its Richter scale is yet strong enough to cause visible cracks in the fabric of Soviet atheism, but the monitors are openly worried about what might be happening to undermine the substructure. There is no single epicentre to draw the attention of the observers in the Kremlin, but they need a thousand eyes to see the small signals coming from every direction at once.

Some of the tinier ethnic groups (in the Baltic States) emit as strong a signal as the larger (the Ukrainians). Modern Soviet youth receive a hundred stimuli to distract them from the conformity of Marxist-Leninist orthodoxy. The lure of foreign culture beckons ever more insistently, the more so because young people cannot travel outside the Soviet Union. Christian rock music may be only a small element in this, but it is distinctly there and growing.

Revival seems to have penetrated Estonia first, which has been able for nearly 30 years to receive Finnish television (in Finnish—a language close enough for the Estonians to understand). Christian rock music was one of the sparks which set alight the Methodist Church in Tallinn, the capital, in the early 1970s. The state moved in brutally and tried to dowse the flame, expelling young people from school and institute. Herbert Murd, the manager of a group called 'Ezra', secretly recorded 'The Milky Way', with lyrics by a Lutheran pastor, Andres Põder, and music by a composer who was notable in his own right.

Murd's experience was devastating for him personally: arrest, imprisonment, mental torture, renunciation of his activities. But the flame had too strong a hold. The youth revival of the Christian faith was underway, and the shower of sparks alighted to find tinder in other places. Such an experience will be one of the recurring themes of this book.

A Backward Glance

Estonia is a tiny country of north-eastern Europe, bounded on the north by the Gulf of Finland, on the east by Russia, on the south by Latvia and on the west by the Gulf of Riga and the Baltic Sea. To visitors it looks like Scandinavia, with its 1,500 inland lakes and 800 islands. It is low-lying, nowhere more than 1,000 feet above sea level. It has a population of approximately 1½ million.

Estonia has known more than its share of foreign domination. Throughout the nineteenth century it was firmly under the control of the Russian Empire, yet never became russianised. The two Russian revolutions in 1905 and 1917, and the subsequent seizure of power by the Communists in November 1917 in Petrograd (Leningrad), which subjugated so many, paradoxically brought independence to Estonia. Before the close of the decade Estonia had managed to appoint a provisional government and declare its independence, but in fighting to make the declaration a reality following the invasion of the country by the Red Army in November 1918, the Estonian army suffered heavy losses, as well as inflicting some in its turn. In February 1920 a peace treaty with the Soviet Union was signed at Tartu. By its terms Russia 'voluntarily and forever' renounced its sovereign rights over the territory and people of Estonia.

After two decades of independence, Estonia claimed

neutrality at the outbreak of the Second World War, but in vain. The Soviet Union and Germany had signed a secret pact dividing Europe between them, as a consequence of which the Soviet Union subjugated Estonia in June 1940, only to be driven out a year later by the Germans. First, however, Estonia became *de facto* a republic of the Soviet Union. To mark this event there were deportations of at least 40,000 Estonians, including politicians, civil servants, army officers, industrialists and bankers, not to mention clergy of all denominations. As thousands were also murdered, Estonian life—political, cultural and religious—was decapitated.

After the German invasion, Estonia suffered a different form of repression and more severe losses. By September 1944 the Soviet Army had regained the territory. The deportations, stopped short by the German occupation, began again. From such a tiny nation, the loss of 20,000 people in 1945–46 and a further 40,000 in 1949 was devastating. It was the flower of the nation, present and future, which suffered. The population of Estonia fell by approximately 15 per cent, a figure that takes into account the number of deportees and those who escaped to the West. The removal of native Estonians from positions of leadership and influence in every walk of life was undoubtedly part of a long-term strategy to place and retain Russians firmly in power in the republic and to recruit and elevate to office only those unrepresentative Estonians who pledged their total allegiance to the Soviet regime.

Church and State
How did these events affect the church and religious life of the country? In 1934 more than 78 per cent of the population belonged to the Lutheran Church and 19 per cent to the Orthodox Church (under Russian nineteenth-century influence). In other words, the two largest confessions before the war claimed the allegiance, at least nominally, of

98 per cent of all Estonians. However, these churches had only just over 20 years (1917–1940) under independent Estonian leadership. Before 1917 their leadership had been firmly in the hands of Germans and Russians respectively.

After 1940 no normal development was possible because of the Soviet takeover. The period of independence was too short for churches to develop a native Estonian tradition. The Estonian Orthodox Church found itself in a very difficult position because in 1945 it became a diocese of the Moscow Patriarchate, whereas before it had enjoyed virtual independence. The extreme resentment felt by the Estonian people towards the Russians because of the annexation of their country gave rise to a struggle to preserve Estonian language, culture and tradition which directly affected all the non-Orthodox Christian denominations. These churches were looked upon by some as organisations where 'the Russians had no say' and thus as positive forces for the survival of the Estonian people.

Given the very high level of allegiance to the Christian faith in Estonia, the Soviet leadership had to introduce measures to try to weaken the impact of the church on the lives of ordinary people: in Soviet terminology, to 're-educate' them and to provide a more attractive alternative to the Christian faith. The Soviet authorities had by this time gained considerable experience to help them in their struggle against religion.

One of the important elements in the re-education programme in Estonia, as elsewhere in the Soviet Union, was the introduction of state-propagated rituals to replace church festivals. For example, in 1957 'summer youth days' were introduced in an attempt to entice young people away from confirmation classes held by the Lutheran and Orthodox churches.[1] These had always been extremely popular and the level of participation in them high. Atheist sources reveal that in 1957 virtually half of all 18-year-olds still took part in confirmation. The 'summer youth days' got off to a slow start, with only 39 participants in the first year, but later they achieved considerable success, growing to 4,000 by 1965, or nearly one third of the relevant age-group. It takes large expenditure on theatre, music and excursions to make the camps that attractive. They culminate in a coming-of-age ceremony at which young people appear in black suits and white dresses just as for church confirmation. Naturally the camps are not simply to provide the young people with a good time: they are also a school of Communism.

Further attempts to outdo church ceremonies were made by a 'Commission for Preparation of New Family Rites' which was founded in 1959 in Tartu. These included the reintroduction of old folk-customs at weddings: the recruitment of musicians specifically to perform at registry offices, the publication of a book entitled 'Songs for Family Occasions' which contains 66 melodies, including 20 for weddings. The ceremony of 'name-giving' was introduced to replace baptism. The first secular funeral ceremony incorporating new rites was held in Tartu in 1960. A special official visits the family of the deceased, discusses the details of the ceremony, arranges for a suitable speaker and hires an orchestra for the funeral procession.

Apart from the introduction of these new secular rituals which have been applied with various adaptations throughout the entire Soviet Union, the war against religion has continued in the usual forms, such as the publication of atheist lectures, atheist propaganda in schools and in the mass media and the formation of atheist societies—already outlined in the introduction. There is also the inevitable direct discrimination against believers in higher education and employment, the use of moral pressure and outright provocation.

How successful has the government been in eradicating the faith in Estonia? If one looks at official statistics and sources in the Soviet period, it seems that the measures taken have had a degree of success.

In an article published in *Questions of Scientific Atheism* in 1972 entitled 'Anti-religious rites in Estonia', a Soviet author claims that religious practice is declining fast. In 10 years the number of baptisms had fallen from over 50 to 12 per cent, and the number of confirmations has fallen from over 10,000 to under 500 in the same period.[2] He describes the success of many of the new ceremonies but has to admit that not all is quite so rosy from the state's point of view: 'There still exist many churches and prayer houses in Estonia, and the clergy are doing everything in their power to keep people under their influence...' He goes on to say that '40 per cent of all funerals in Estonia are still church events to this day'.[3]

The statistics in such articles, of which there are many in the Soviet press, are coloured by the needs of propaganda, but even so the authors cannot disguise the resilience of religion. More than a decade after this article appeared, there is evidence of greater vitality of the faith in Estonia, rather than less, even though the pressure against it is more concerted. To illustrate that, we will look further at the Estonian Methodists, one of the Soviet Union's smallest and least-known churches.

A Small Christian Group

Finland was part of the Russian Empire in the second half of the nineteenth century, when it provided the channel through which Methodism first gained entry.[4] A Methodist society was founded in St Petersburg in 1889, a member of which was an Estonian lay preacher, who returned home to begin Methodist work there in 1907. The first Methodist society was founded in 1910 on Estonia's largest island, Saaremaa, where two years later the first church was erected. By the Second World War there were societies in 13 other towns.

The Estonian Methodist Church had its own periodical *Kristlik Kaitsja* (Christian Defender) which was founded in 1920 and appeared monthly until it ceased in 1940, never to be resumed. There were 26 Sunday schools, and a Methodist youth club was founded in 1920. These and other scattered churches in the Baltic States maintained close links both with the Methodist leadership in Sweden and with the Methodists in America.

The Methodist Church in Estonia is now the only one remaining in the Soviet Union and is part of the Northern Europe district (one of the four European episcopal districts of the United Methodist Church) under Bishop Ole Borgen (Stockholm). For several years immediately after the re-occupation of Estonia by the Russians, the Methodist Church there was out of contact with its leadership in Sweden and in the USA. At this time it reported only 750 members. One of the first signs that the Soviet regime recognised the legality of the Methodist Church was the publication of a sermon on peace by the Methodist superintendent at one of the post-war peace conferences held in Zagorsk. In subsequent years Alexander Kuum—now in his eighties and Superintendent Emeritus of the Estonian Methodist Church—represented his church at general conferences of the UMC in America.

In the post-war era the Estonian Methodist Church has grown dramatically to 2,200 in 15 congregations, the largest of which is in Tallinn, the capital city. The Tallinn church has a particularly interesting history. Survival alone would have been a miracle, but its growth and revival are even more extraordinary. Before a description of its life on the basis of accounts written by its own ministers and by visitors from the West, it is worth mentioning another article published in the official Soviet publication, *Questions of Scientific Atheism* in 1979.[5] The author gives a brief history of the rise of Methodism in Estonia, chronicles the fortunes of this church in the post-war period and describes in a surprisingly objective and accurate way the characteristic features of its forms of worship, pastoral work and evangelism.

In the article a tension can clearly be felt between the need to admonish complacent Communist activists for not doing enough to counteract the obvious achievements of the Methodists and the necessity to minimise the effect and influence of the Methodist Church, portraying it as a body struggling to survive against impossible odds because of the success of atheist education and the spread of a materialist world-view. If one had only this one article as a source of information about Methodism in Estonia, it would provide adequate testimony to a full and lively church life.

The author explains the rapid growth in membership of the Estonian Methodist Church in the following way:

During the post-war period the basic aim of the Estonian Methodist Churches was to strive to adapt to contemporary reality, to reinforce the ranks of believers by means of active missionary recruitment and to find new ways of deepening the religious experience of believers ... all their activities were geared to these ends. There were some achievements. One should note first of all the increase in the number of adherents of the Methodist Church. Between 1943 and 1973 membership increased from 1,242 to 2,300.[6]

Acknowledging such church growth is virtually unprecedented in a Soviet source. The author attributes it mainly to the transfer of believers to the Methodist Church from other religious groups, such as Lutherans and Baptists. This explanation is partially valid, because several small non-conformist groups, such as the Salvation Army, were banned after the Soviet take-over.

However, this explanation cannot be the whole truth because the Baptists were experiencing rapid growth at the same time. The atheist account misses out the key factor in the post-war growth of the Tallinn Methodist Church: the preaching and ministry of Hugo Oengo. An engineer by profession, he combined his expertise on bridges with his Christian work after the Soviet occupation, refusing to renounce his faith under intense pressure in the Stalinist period. His resolution stimulated the revival. He rarely had the time for preparation which a full-time minister would

have had, but his spirituality shone out from behind all
obstacles, especially while the official pastor, Alexander
Kuum, was in Siberian exile. Later he did give up his secular work, and after Pastor Kuum returned home the two together formed a ministry of great power and effectiveness.

Hugo Oengo gave this modest account of these years:

Before the war, in 1940, there were two Methodist churches in
Tallinn, with fewer than 300 adult members. The large church
building with 1,000 seats was destroyed in the war and both
congregations met in the small chapel, with 150 seats. The usual
attendance was only 40–60 people. The small group began to pray
for revival. After the first campaign, membership rose to 170, and
that was at the end of 1945. In 1950 another church building with
500 seats was made available to us. After another prayer campaign, the number of members at the end of 1953 was more than
300. After a third campaign, the number of members grew to
1,000 by the end of 1962, including a small group of Pentecostals
who had united with the Methodists. In nine years we had gained
700 members.[7]

Alexander Kuum further reported that by 1965 the
membership in Estonia as a whole had grown to 2,100,
excluding as many again who worshipped regularly but did
not become full members.

Hugo Oengo wrote that in the late 1960s and early 1970s
the membership evened off. The building, rented from the
Adventists, contained only 500 seats; so extra services had
to be held to accommodate all who wished to worship, and
'only the Lord knows what we should do next'.

The 'atheist' article indicates the reaction of the church
to the slowing down of its growth:

The third conference of the Estonian Methodist Church took
place on 23 March 1968 in Tallinn and it was no accident that the
leader of the Methodist Church, Superintendent A Kuum, expressed his alarm. 'We must pray for enlightenment and for a
reawakening, because we have been transformed from a growing
church into a dying church. Growth in the past three years has

been small, but we hope that this is merely a temporary phenomenon.'[8]

The atheist source goes on to give an unusually frank insight into the methods of evangelism the church adopted:

As if in response to this appeal, the believers began to organise activities intended to revive the church and to strengthen its ranks. For example, they held regular campaigns which they called 'revival weeks', usually in autumn or winter, especially to recruit new members. During these weeks more trained preachers appeared in the churches, collections were taken to meet financial needs and refreshments were provided for those who attended.[9]

The same article illustrates how the Methodist leaders kept new converts in the church:

The system of 'classes' was introduced at the dawn of Methodism and has retained its significance even today. Usually the class consists of 10–12 members and the leader is chosen from among a number of more experienced Methodists. The leader is obliged to meet each member of his class every week, to enquire about his spiritual progress, to give advice, to exhort, comfort or encourage according to circumstances and to receive gifts for the support of the preachers, the church and the poor.[10]

The author further reveals that if the behaviour or attitude of a member of the class causes concern, the class leader has to inform the preacher or minister. If the wayward member is not willing to subject him or herself to church discipline then the person concerned will be expelled. Such a person may only be readmitted to membership following repentance and a sincere promise not to cause trouble in the future and to lead an exemplary Christian life. Class leaders are described as being 'experienced believers who observe the lives and level of spirituality of their class members, paying particular attention to their needs and spiritual problems and where necessary offering them moral and material support'. Each member of the class is obligated to 'spread religion among non-believers and reinforce the ranks of the Methodist Church'. In conclusion, the author states: 'The existence of the classes and the fairly flexible and capable management of them is one of the main reasons for the viability and activity of the Estonian Methodist Church'.

The author goes on to pick out various other features of the life of the church and in particular gives a detailed account of the various types of church service, the content of sermons, prayers, the musical aspects of worship, the attitudes of young and older believers which, when taken as a whole, convey a very attractive picture of the life of the church. It seems that the author cannot help admiring the effective witness of the church. About church services he writes:

The form and theme of the service are widely varied. Apart from the normal worship there are 'revival services'. These are intended mainly for non-believers, waverers and young members of the church. There are also 'Bible hours', devoted to the exposition of specific biblical principles, and thanksgiving services. In the Tallinn church on Thursdays there are services specifically aimed at young people...
A distinctive feature of the Methodist services is the so-called introductory prayer time. Before the beginning of the service the deacons collect written declarations from the congregation with specific requests for prayers. The number of such petitions, for example, at the Tallinn church, is between 20 and 25. About 50 per cent of the requests for prayer concern the health of the believers and their relatives, 20 per cent are prayers for strengthening the faith or for the conversion to the faith of relatives and acquaintances, 15 per cent concern family problems and the rest are about various other matters, for example, housing or education. The preachers accord great significance to these prayers. If someone recovers from an illness or a difficult situation is resolved, then it is imperative to thank God for the answer and to refer to it as a concrete example of answered prayer.[11]

The author even comments on the vitality of the music

used in worship. It is very different according to the generation being addressed. Older people prefer 'traditional songs and familiar melodies', while 'for the young people they have introduced a modern repertoire, which includes modern jazz rhythms'. The atheist writer doubts the success of these methods, but we know of their effectiveness from independent Christian sources, as we indicated at the beginning of this chapter.

The author then goes on to identify the central importance of the sermon. Even those without theological training make up for this by their experience. All preachers adapt their words to the specific needs and concerns of their particular congregations. He continues:

There are special sermons at missionary services, for example at the Tallinn church, attended by people who are not members of it, which embrace a wide range of religious and secular problems. In such sermons, known as 'proclamations of the Gospel', the role of salvation through faith during the mortal life of the individual is emphasised. Believers are called upon to attain holiness, to fulfil all the biblical commandments, to do good, to refuse to do evil deeds. The thread which runs through the whole sermon is the necessity to love God without reservation.

Moral teaching also falls into this category. Here, traditional sermons in which temperance is lauded and alcoholism condemned occupy a central position. Great attention is also paid to Christian marriage, to the family and upbringing of children. Reference is often made to a leading Christian personality and how his views and convictions were formed. The preachers emphasise the leading role of education in the family and the influence of Christian parents.[12]

This article is one of the liveliest and most attractive accounts of Christian life ever to have appeared in a Soviet source; our knowledge of Estonian Methodism is the richer for it. There is very little in it which even begins to suggest that the Tallinn church is in decline.

Recent Testimony

Although Christian writing in the Soviet Union is extensively suppressed, the Methodist leaders in Tallinn have been able occasionally to produce circular letters—significantly, in English, and so designated for foreign consumption.

In the first of the two in the Keston College Archive (actually numbered 75), Alexander Kuum describes a solemn moment in the life of the Tallinn community—the death of Hugo Oengo in March 1978. His funeral service took place in the large Baptist church (known as Oleviste), as the Methodist church was too small. This in itself is a rare example of permitted ecumenical co-operation in Soviet conditions. Thousands of people flocked to it, including representatives of the government's Council on Religious Affairs, the body which controls relations between church and state. Christians of other denominations showed their high regard for him by attending; there was even a delegation from the Finnish Methodist Church. Fifty wreaths were laid on his grave at the cemetery. One cannot help noticing the irony: the church funeral of a respected Christian leader is attended by representatives of an atheist government which had devoted a great deal of its time and energy, as we have seen, to the eradication of Christian rites and the introduction of secular ones.

The rest of Pastor Kuum's circular letter concentrates mainly on contacts between the Estonian Methodists and foreign visitors, with some reference to internal ecumenical relations. In order to achieve this 'normality' some compromise with the system is essential. Herein lies a key problem for every pastor and priest in the Soviet Union: where does legitimate accommodation smudge into the area of compromise of the faith? How far should Christians stand out and obey the Pauline injunction not to be 'conformed' to this world, but to be 'transformed' (Rom 12:2)? How far, on the other hand, should one be prepared to render unto

Caesar what is Caesar's? Nowhere do these two apparently contradictory questions find sharper focus than in the two chapters on Estonia which open this book.

The compromise is seen most clearly in the type of statements Estonian Methodists—and other Soviet Christians—write for foreign consumption in an official capacity. Of course, there are genuinely good and positive things to say about the life of Soviet churches, but at the same time it is impossible for Christians officially to speak or write freely about the problems they encounter because of state control of religious activities and the secularisation of Soviet society. It would be unthinkable for them to criticise government policy, except in private. This often gives rise, unfortunately, to ambiguity and misunderstanding. There is a tendency in what the Methodists write to give undue emphasis to their somewhat meagre privileges and freedoms. The mention, for example, of extensive foreign travel in the circular letter may sound propagandistic and give the impression of greater freedom than actually exists, but the development of such foreign contacts is nevertheless an element in the growth of the church.

Alexander Kuum reports ecumenical contacts throughout 1978 which indicate, at least at leadership level, that the Methodists maintain good relations with other Christian denominations. For example, Kuum and Heigo Ritsbek, then secretary of the Tallinn Church, were guests of the Russian Orthodox Church in Moscow and Zagorsk for the sixtieth anniversary of the restoration of the Patriarchate. Pastor Kuum preached at a service of the Tallinn Lutheran Church during a week of ecumenical prayer. Highlights of the year in the Methodist Church itself were the celebration in March 1978 of the 60th anniversary of the founding of Haapsalu Methodist Church in 1918 and a special meeting on evangelism held in the Tallinn church from 12–15 October in accordance with the World Methodist Council plan on evangelism. The Methodist Church also made a contribution to 'peace work'. A 'peace meeting' was held at

Haapsalu Methodist Church in August. Pastor Olav Pärnamets attended a peace meeting of all religious organisations in the USSR in Moscow and in 1978 the Methodist Church in Estonia contributed 1,000 roubles for the Peace Fund (45 kopecks for each Estonian Methodist—about 45p, but at least four times this in value when comparative wages are considered).

In conclusion, Pastor Kuum gives some statistics for 1978–79 for all the Methodist churches in Estonia. In 1978 there were almost 3,000 worship services with just under 300,000 attendances, of which over 200 were services of Holy Communion.

We do not, unfortunately, learn very much about the personality of Alexander Kuum from this rather impersonal circular letter for which, quite clearly, he writes according to a prescribed formula. But because he is now a very old man (84 in 1986), he can look back over a life which has been dedicated to serving the Methodist Church and reflect on some considerable achievements—given the difficulties of surviving as a Christian in an atheist society where so many restrictions are placed on the life of the church. In 1983 he was honoured for his service to the Methodist Church when he was awarded the 1983 'Upper Room' citation. This was the first time since the initiation of this award in Nashville, Tennessee, that anyone from an Eastern bloc country had received it.

The second circular letter, dated May 1979, by Pastor Pärnamets, is totally different in approach and style from the one by Alexander Kuum and, it must be said, is much more lively and interesting. Undoubtedly this is a reflection of a younger personality who, on the evidence of this letter, is much more concerned about conveying something positive about the Christian faith than satisfying the official censor. Unfortunately no more have been published. The letter is plainly intended to encourage and inspire fellow Christians, whether in the Soviet Union or abroad.

He begins by writing in a warm and personal way about

the death of Hugo Oengo and referring to the great loss experienced by the whole church because of it. But he concludes: 'God has promised to be with us forever. This is a real comfort in our grief'. The introduction of a simple biblical truth as a means of encouraging fellow Christians is typical of his approach. He then refers to the fact that the Conference of the Methodist Church in Estonia held in March 1979 appointed him Superintendent, and he asks his fellow Christians to pray for him. He then gives a brief autobiography which reads in full:

I have been connected with the Methodist Church in Estonia since my conversion in November 1951, when I was 14 years old. I remember that prayer meeting in Tallinn Methodist Church under the leadership of the Rev Alexander Kuum. At the end of the service, he, having very joyful countenance, asked a simple but very important question: 'Who wants to accept Jesus Christ as his personal Saviour?' There was heated fight in my heart. But Jesus won the victory. I stood up and said, 'I do.' We prayed. God's peace filled my heart. This experience has endured for 28 years. Besides, I must state the fact that after my conversion there was a great and positive change in my life.

In 1966 I was appointed as the minister at a little Methodist church in Paide (a small town 55 miles from Tallinn). In 1970 I was appointed to the Tallinn Methodist Church. I have had the privilege of serving the church that has been so great a blessing to me. I cannot count all these blessings, but one of them is my wife Urve. We were married in 1962 and have three daughters, Kersti, Ulle and Eve, and a baby son, Andres.[13]

In conclusion, Pastor Pärnamets mentions a visit made by Bishop Ole Borgen of Sweden, representing the United Methodist Church North European District, in March 1979. He points out that this was the bishop's fourth visit to Tallinn, but on this occasion he was able to visit Methodist churches outside the capital in Tartu, Pärnu and Paide. During this visit he consecrated Pastor Pärnamets as Superintendent of the Methodist Church in Estonia and ordained four men as deacons in the Tallinn church and two as deacons at the Tartu church.

Heigo Ritsbek is a younger leader of the community, obviously acceptable to the Soviet authorities for advancement in leadership. He was born in 1951 and, having graduated in history from the University of Tartu, was one of the deacons whom Bishop Borgen ordained in 1979. As a fluent English speaker, he has developed many personal contacts with visitors and is now second minister of the Tallinn church. He has been host, for example, to the Rev David Bridge of the British Methodist Division of Home Mission, who has paid a number of visits to the church in Tallinn. He and his family were there over Christmas in 1984, and he published an account of his visit.[14] Mr Bridge reinforces what we know of the vitality and witness of the Tallinn church.

We are immediately reminded of the great significance of the sermon in a Methodist service, described in *Questions of Scientific Atheism* as 'occupying a prominent place in the ideological arsenal of the Estonian Methodists'. Mr Bridge had come to Tallinn expecting to be asked to preach once and he had, with foresight, prepared a second sermon to hold 'in reserve'. Having met up with his long-standing friend Olav Pärnamets and his wife and children on arrival in Tallinn, he was informed that he would be called upon to preach five times in the next three days. Mr Bridge commented:

Idle to protest that the congregation would rather hear from their own minister at Christmas time for I know they will be doing this anyway. A service with only one sermon would be considered merely as an aperitif by the Tallinn Methodists. Nor can I resolve the problem by preaching only half a sermon at a time. Anything less than half an hour will be regarded as a greeting and welcomed only as an addition to and not a substitute for a sermon. There is no alternative but to stay up tonight until three more sermons are written.[15]

The family's first full day in Tallinn was 23rd December, a Sunday, and the first service of the day was 10am. Heigo Ritsbek interpreted for Mr Bridge. About 650 people were present in the congregation (the building seats only 500). This was followed at 12.30pm by a Russian language service and at 3pm by a youth service (this is one of those rare Soviet churches permitted such activities). After a short break the Bridge family were taken to a church social evening where everyone shared a meal together and was involved in performing various musical items.

There is no official holiday for Christmas in the Soviet Union (not even for Orthodox Christmas two weeks later). On Christmas Eve the evening service is one of the greatest occasions in the Christian year for Estonians. Afterwards people go home to share the main Christmas event, a celebratory family meal and the exchange of gifts. The Bridge family joined the Pärnamets family and they experienced 'one of the happiest Christmas Eves we can remember'.

At the morning service on Christmas Day the congregation of just under 500 comprised mainly retired people. However, the evening service was a rather special event, aimed principally at non-believers. There was a great emphasis on music, with several different choirs taking part separately and all joining together at the end. The Tallinn church has 12 different music groups—separate choirs for Estonian and Russian services, a male-voice choir, a ladies' choir, a chamber-music choir, three choirs (one Russian) using folk instruments, a symphony orchestra, a trumpet group and two modern music groups (one Russian). At this service there was only one sermon and no collection. Mr Bridge described the atmosphere as follows:

The church is packed out—quite the largest congregation we have seen on this visit and though this is the fifth service of the Christmas season, no one seems anxious to get away early. At intervals people appear with trays of biscuits, sweets and fruit. Surely the love feast in the Early Church must have been not unlike this. It is nine o'clock before the benediction is pronounced, but in the whole of the three hours I do not feel bored for a moment. Why is that? Most of all I think because everyone is so obviously glad to be here. It means so much to them to be part of the church family, the joy they feel is shared easily with others.[16]

On the following day Mr Bridge and Pastor Pärnamets had an appointment with the Deputy Secretary of State for Religious Affairs in Estonia, Kalja Oja. This was obviously an opportunity for Mr Bridge to raise various, perhaps slightly thorny, issues of importance for the well-being and for the ongoing witness of the Methodist Church in Estonia. Top of the list was the question of the provision of theological education. The Methodist Church has no theological college nor even a correspondence course; permission for Methodist ministers to study abroad has not been forthcoming. Mr Bridge mentioned to Mr Oja the forthcoming World Methodist Peace assembly to be held in London in August 1985 and suggested that Mr Pärnamets should be given permission to attend as a representative of his country (which he was able to do). Finally Mr Bridge broached the subject of a possible visit to Tallinn by a group of British Methodists in 1986. Mr Oja, whom Mr Bridge described as both courteous and well informed, reacted favourably to this suggestion and even agreed to meet such a delegation and speak to them about the place of the Church in a socialist society. The visit was duly planned for Easter 1986 and oversubscribed by British Methodists, but this did not prevent its subsequent cancellation by the Soviet authorities.

Despite all the positive signs of the vigour of the Tallinn church, Mr Bridge also remarked that, in his opinion, it did not seem as crowded as it had done on previous visits. This impression of a slight falling off in numbers was confirmed by Pastor Pärnamets, who has reported that the number of young people now joining the church is not balancing the heavy losses due to the death of elderly members of the congregation. The present figures for formal church membership indicate that the church has not actually been growing in numbers in the past five years, but growth that is not reflected in them may still be occurring.

Taking the Soviet Union as a whole, there has been a marked deterioration in the fortunes of religious believers since 1979. While there is no evidence to suggest that any of the wide-ranging activities of the Methodists as outlined in this chapter have been curtailed or restricted, it is likely that the general climate of increased oppression, a fact of life during Brezhnev's last years and under Andropov, Chernenko and now Gorbachov, has had some impact on the life of the Methodist Church in Estonia. It is probable that many young people in 1986, while confessing and living out the Christian faith, will not go as far as to enrol as church members for fear of jeopardising their educational and career prospects. If they do not enrol, they are naturally not included in church statistics, but this does not necessarily mean that the church as a whole has stopped growing or has ceased to be effective in its evangelism. A similar phenomenon can be seen in other Christian circles in the Soviet Union. There is great dedication to the faith among young Orthodox intellectuals, for example, but many of them prefer to keep a low profile to the extent of not even attending the liturgy, but meeting secretly in small groups in people's homes for discussion and Bible study.

Another factor undoubtedly affecting the growth in the Methodist Church is healthy competition from other churches. In some places (see Chapter 2) there are the first signs of a revival in the traditional Lutheran Church. The Oleviste Baptist Church in Tallinn is thriving and is currently attracting scores of young people to its spacious and convenient premises. Loyalty to a particular denomination is likely to be less pronounced among the present generation of young people who have been born and educated during the Soviet period. By contrast, men and women who were born during Estonia's brief independence between the two world wars, now in their fifties and sixties and who perhaps attended Methodist Sunday schools and were involved in Methodist youth work, naturally remember the 'good old days' and their allegiance to Christ *and* Methodism is far more pronounced. Younger people without this tradition behind them would have few qualms about going off to explore other churches and transferring their affiliation to another church if they deemed that it had more to offer them spiritually or in other ways.

Where does Pastor Pärnamets stand in all this? During August 1985 while he was in Britain attending the World Methodist Peace Assembly he spoke of the need, both in Britain and Estonia, to re-examine the ideals of the founder of Methodism, John Wesley:

My feeling is that we, both in Estonia and Britain, do not have the same fire in our hearts to save souls, to preach the Gospel with the life-changing love and power as John Wesley and others did in their generation ... But we are not a hopeless people—God can do it again when we pray ... The Lord wants to give us revival, but sometimes we have become so lukewarm and formalistic and lifeless so that when the Lord sends revival we do not recognise it— but we must be ready to accept new life when the Lord decides to give it.[17]

Such a sign of that revival is the Christian rock music with which we began this chapter. The key group—and the first in the Soviet Union—was founded by Janus Karner in 1969, under the name 'Selah' (a musical direction in the Psalms that indicates a musical interlude). Ezra was merely one of its several offshoots, which came into being not only in Estonia, but even as far afield as Leningrad (Valeri Barinov's 'Trumpet Call' group), Georgia and Armenia. Selah has, not surprisingly, come under immense pressure from the Soviet authorities.

It was not easy, either, for older church members to accept these new ways of worshipping God, but the pastors did not exclude them, despite the pressures, and they have contributed to renewal in a small church which could well have days of even greater growth ahead of it.

Chapter 2

Estonian Lutherans: Growth Through Preaching

'Please be seated.' At the end of the hymn before the sermon preachers around the world utter some such phrase to settle the congregation in their pews. This time they stayed standing. 'Please be seated,' he said again, more loudly this time. No one moved. The Rev Harri Mõtsnik, Estonian preacher extraordinary, delivered the whole of his sermon at Urvaste that day, 11th November 1984, to a packed congregation which remained on its feet in his honour. It was his farewell to them as their pastor, his last time in the pulpit before facing imprisonment, maybe even torture. He had been with them a mere three years, but in that time not only had local people come to love him as a man, but many people had begun to flock in from neighbouring places in the south of Estonia and even from more distant areas of the country to hear his sensational preaching, and this was happening in that very Lutheran Church in the Baltic States which had for 40 years seemed—at least to the outside observer—the only Christian Church in the whole Soviet Union which has failed to make significant gains in the recent battle against atheism.

It may seem eccentric to begin this study of Christian growth in the Soviet Union with not one, but two examples from Estonia, the smallest of the 15 Soviet republics, and geographically this criticism may be justified. However, Estonia has received far less attention than many other areas of the Soviet Union, and signs of a Lutheran revival affect not only neighbouring Latvia, but also areas of Soviet Central Asia, where church growth is also occurring among Lutheran churches planted in post-war years.

From Lawyer to Pastor

Harri Mõtsnik's biography is unique for a pastor in the Soviet Union. He was born into a simple Christian farming family in the countryside, on 5th September 1928, when Estonia was a free country (see p 21–22). The succession of Soviet, German and then again Soviet invasions came for him between the most impressionable ages of 11 and 16. Most Estonians born around that period became patriots, and many suffered for their commitment at some later stage. But Pastor Mõtsnik's stirring activity began at a time when, on the surface, Estonia had long seemed 'pacified' into one more Soviet republic.

The truth is that many years of his early maturity were occupied with his practice of the law, in which he had graduated from Tartu University. We know nothing of his life in this profession, but his conversion came through the gift of a Bible from abroad. A pastor in Finland commissioned one of his congregation, due to travel to Estonia, to give a Bible to someone whom he met. Harri Mõtsnik was the eventual recipient, and it 'stopped me on my journey'—the phrase he later used in a sermon. It is virtually impossible for a mature man in the Soviet Union to abandon the prominence of a professional career in order to join a theological seminary. For Harri Mõtsnik there was one factor which made it slightly easier: the theological institute in Tallinn was not fully residential. Most of its instruction was by correspondence course, and the students only now and then gathered for communal activities. Therefore no new residence permits were necessary and there was less surveillance. Sadly, his wife could not go along with his courageous decision to abandon his first career—a fact which the Soviets later exploited. She left him, but he has maintained contact with his son and daughter.

From 1970, at the age of 42, Harri Mõtsnik became an assistant pastor, being ordained and acquiring his own parish two years later. His third appointment, in 1976, was to an influential post: one of the very few Lutheran parishes on Russian soil, at Pushkin, near Leningrad. Here his outstanding Christian work was in a place where he could begin to become known internationally and could meet foreign Christians from time to time. The inevitable corollary of this was harassment by the KGB. 'There I learned what kind of ruthless control governs spiritual life,' he said later.

He was referring to the severe Soviet controls over parish life, introduced by Khrushchev in 1961, which reduced the pastor to the status of employee of the parish council of three lay people. Unlike the Russian Orthodox Church, Lutherans never fully accepted this and fought secretly to keep the pastor as their head. The state retaliated against the strong opposition which Pastor Mõtsnik led in Leningrad. There was a systematic series of robberies in his church, for which believers themselves received the blame, while it was obvious that the authorities were responsible. Up to this point Pastor Mõtsnik had acted with discretion, but now he became a fearless fighter.

He felt he would be less exposed back in his homeland, and so in 1981 took up an appointment at Urvaste, in the south of Estonia in an isolated region not significantly penetrated by foreign influences and where many vigorous pastors are active.

Here, due to his dedication and outspokenness, his ministry flourished over the next three years. As he was clearing out decades of rubbish from an abandoned old chapel in the cemetery there, he reflected on the sad falling away from the Lutheran Church in his homeland, asking himself, 'Has God really been forgotten in Urvaste?' His preaching, which became the distinctive mark of his Christian ministry, rapidly demonstrated to the whole Estonian nation that the answer was 'no'.

Pastor Mõtsnik's training in law helped to make him a commanding and forthright figure in the pulpit. There are not many men in the Soviet Union who have abandoned oratory in a court of law to become preachers. As we know from a collection of them published in Sweden in 1986, his sermons were eloquent, authoritative and to the point. It is from this booklet that almost all the information in this chapter originates.

In his new post the attentions of the KGB were directed more at his person than at the church building, as they had been in Russia. The campaign of the atheist authorities against him was unrelenting. The booklet mentioned above, entitled *What is Needed for Peace?* concludes with evidence of the precise nature of this harassment. It is a transcript, made by Pastor Mõtsnik himself just after the event, of a threatening 'interview' with a representative of the KGB in 1983.

The officer begins by asking him why he mentioned in a sermon the shooting down of the Korean airliner (which had just occurred). Pastor Mõtsnik replied that Christianity obliges one to uphold the sacredness of life and to tell the truth. If this is not done, it makes it all the easier to go on to further and bigger crimes.

Ironically, considering that he was a lawyer, he was next grilled on whether he was familiar with the laws which regulate religious life in the Soviet Union. His reply showed not only the expected keen knowledge of them, but also sharp criticism:

The law forbidding religious instruction to children is a reproach to the Soviet state and to atheism ... they are taught lies instead of truth.[1]

Pastor Mõtsnik went on to illustrate the shocking way in which the authorities were treating Estonian children. On Christmas Eve a music teacher brought her pupils to Urvaste church to hear carols and organ music. For this their behaviour assessment was marked down to fail and the school forced the children to write denunciations of the teacher, after which she was dismissed.

The interrogator turned the conversation to the USA, and after hearing the pastor's opinon that the situation was better there than in the USSR, he warned him insistently of dismissal if he continued to be 'involved in politics'.

A year later the threats became reality. Further pastoral work became impossible. Pastor Mõtsnik relinquished his parish after preaching his final sermon and sought peace in the countryside of his birthplace (Varbla), where for a few months he gleaned a simple livelihood by tending a flock of sheep. His arrest came five months later, on 3rd April 1985.

The Preacher

Those who know Harri Mõtsnik say he was, at the outset, shy and timid. In being forced to preach, he found strength from God, his resolve hardened by the tactics and intrigues of the KGB. It is not surprising, when one reviews the content of these sermons, to learn of their electric effect. The Soviet system treats non-Russian nationalism even more harshly than it does the religious revival. The two in combination form a mixture which is all the more potent because they can exist officially nowhere in public life, yet they express some of the deepest feelings known to man. Pastor Mõtsnik always held the two in balance, never once allowing national sentiments to deface and overlay the essential Christian message. A tiny nation of under 1½ million people is as valuable in the eyes of God, he tells us, as the most populous on earth.

All men are created equal by a loving God. He has blessed the Estonian people once with freedom, counted them as equals among other nations and countries of the world.

The Apostle says: 'You were bought at a price; do not become slaves of men' (I Cor 7:23). The human soul is a creation of God and should not be enslaved by anyone...

Freedom is not loyalty to the state regime in power, if it is not Christian, that is, subordinated to Jesus Christ. He has bought us into freedom once and for all, he has redeemed us.

The truth about existing conditions in the country, about the injustice being done by man to man and the crimes being committed by one country against another—these will all come to light one day.... True freedom can exist only when our land and our people have joined their destinies with Christ and all listen in humility to the voice of Truth.

Freedom always liberates from the old and the bad, while creating conditions for something new and good; truth liberates from self and makes one live for the benefit of others, giving them a space in which to live. By contrast, self-centred freedom leads to a dead end, to narrow-mindedness, to anguish of soul and to tensions with neighbours. It is not right for us to seek escape from our situation by external forms of expression, folk-dancing and music on the zither and accordion, for these are no more than an empty shell. Dishonesty is no substitute for truth, friendship for love of one's neighbour, the secular name-giving ceremony for the sacrament of baptism, erotic young meetings on long summer evenings for confirmation instruction...

It is also blasphemy to emphasise material things and represent them as the accomplishments of men, rather than as the gifts from God which they are. Among these are the right to daily bread, work, peace and a secure life. Experience has shown that totalitarian regimes demand that citizens forgo some of their liberties, such as freedom of thought, speech, choice of place to live, the right to travel and to free association. In these states ideology stands above the ideal of freedom and the laws of God, and it is the state's rules of behaviour that become the norm.

Freedom is not understood or sufficiently valued until it is lost and the realisation of its absence becomes a personal experience. Freedom is not an illusion, but an experience of reality. It is a vital need. It is not out of place to remember the valiant men and women who have chosen the noble path of self-sacrifice rather than self-interest and furthering their own careers; they have chosen the struggle for freedom as the only way of hope for the Estonian people, setting on one side the fear which they surely experience within and in face of the totalitarian regime which confronts them. Truth is their guide along the way.

Martin Luther said: 'The Christian by faith is the lord of all and no one's slave; by love he is no one's lord, but a servant of all.'[2]

In another sermon Harri Mõtsnik reflects on the longing Soviet people have for true peace. This can never come at home while 'true justice has been trodden under foot', nor while Christians are under attack as virtual outcasts, nor while young people are systematically demoralised by being taught no ideals and seduced by the ready availability of cheap vodka.[3] Nor is there peace while young Estonians are despatched as conscripts in the Red Army to fight the rebels in Afghanistan.[4] The focal point of the sermon presented a very clear argument.

Peace is very precious, because it is necessary for life. To a Christian peace means a good and secure life, clean air and water, health and long life. This includes a democratic, independent homeland, freedom of conscience and religion. Like all else, peace is also a gift from God to man .... No peace can exist where the relationship with God is not right, or where the government authority is not under the rule of Christ, for Jesus is the peace of the world...

Peace is global; it should not be distributed selectively among the nations.... I dedicate this sermon to all who are fighting for justice and peace, who are the hope of our nation and all nations which are yearning for freedom and for a better and more just world.[5]

Millions of people in the third world and in South Africa, for instance, would understand such sentiments readily and instinctively. Unfashionable because they emanate from the Soviet Union, they are nevertheless closely in tune with the spirit of the age.

A subject more particular to Soviet conditions, though rarely touched upon in registered churches because of state pressure to avoid it, is religious oppression, that special mark of Soviet Communism.

The Bible, while not forbidden by law, is treated as a subversive book. Every effort is made to block its distribution 'because of the ideals of truth and freedom contained in it'.[6] History is littered with unsuccessful attempts by rulers to destroy the Bible. Diocletian thought he had destroyed all the Bibles in Rome at the beginning of the fourth century, but the next emperor, Constantine the Great, nevertheless found several copies when he wanted to learn of the faith from them, and two of these exist even today.

Atheist education in general and lack of biblical teaching to young people in particular, Pastor Mõtsnik says, has had a deleterious effect on the morals of the younger generation. Atheism is indeed Satanic and the situation in Estonia can never improve until the country is free of it.

A sermon entitled 'Faithfulness and Watchfulness' must surely be the strongest Christian condemnation of the state policy on atheism ever to come from the Soviet Union.[7] It must have been preached in the presence of other Lutheran pastors.

The situation today is in no way better than it was during the time of the Early Church. Satan is watching as always for opportunities to frustrate the work of God. Satan has established his power in our land, subjugated the church and the people to his will, demanding that faith, religious practices and the teaching of religion to children be renounced. All that we fought for, all that was holy and precious, is now designated as a relic of the past. Scientific atheism replaces them—labour for the benefit of Satan, for the building and extending of his kingdom.... The new laws remove the demand to love one's neighbour and any obligation to keep the commands of God. Satan makes only one demand: obedience to himself, his collaborators and his kingship....

A choice lies before Estonian Christians: whether to side with the Anti Christ and adopt a godless way of life—to become the *homo sovieticus*—or to side with Jesus Christ and become God's children and heirs to the Kingdom of Heaven. The choice is stark, and there is no third way. No compromise with Satan is permissible....

No earthly authority can force us to be silent as we declare the truth. When we do so, we must go on to say: 'Here I stand, I can do no other'. These words of Luther are the shield and sword of Lutheran pastors in an atheist society.

As workers in the kingdom of God, we must forgo the comforts of life and our honour; our personal life is freed from all that hinders us from giving ourselves up to God and the service of our neighbour. My advice to you, dear colleagues, is: do not fear Satan; rather fear God. Take strength upon strength from him.... Satan is very crafty. He knows the weaknesses of men and the fears of their heart. Some he entices by medals and fame, others by money and better career opportunities, others by membership of delegations to travel abroad and by holidays at Western resorts. Satan is a well-versed student of human character and approaches each individual according to his personal weaknesses. Do not think that you can fool him while accepting his gifts.

Satan is very angry and atheism is his form of attack. The Cross makes him angry. Observe the signs of the times and mark how the symbol of the Cross is disappearing from daily life: from post cards, from cemeteries. The Cross on the arch of the gate to Urvaste cemetery disappeared one day and has never been found.

Woe to us pastors who spend our time agonising in remorse ... God will not let his people be destroyed.... The lives of our people are in the hand of God. Treasure that and·be thankful to God. Be thankful that atheism has not been able completely to destroy the self-esteem and national consciousness of the Estonians, nor their desire for freedom, nor their faith in God who can make all things new.

These brave and decisive public themes are by no means the only ones which appear in the sermons. He often talks of the intimacy of the family and of personal faith, enlivened by much personal reminiscence and circumstantial detail.

I remember a family in Ingermanland [a small area between Estonia and Leningrad]. It had six children, but it lost its breadwinner through an industrial accident. The widowed mother fell on hard times financially, so that people close to the family became deeply concerned. Life went on, however. The widowed mother was able to work hard and do all the domestic chores as well and the children were properly dressed and fed. They had a small family house under construction when the husband died, but eventually the family was able to occupy it. A miracle had taken place. Friends and acquaintances wanted to know their secret. She told me she would give this answer to anyone who asked—a quotation from the Bible: 'But those who hope in the Lord will renew their strength.' Here was the secret of life for a woman who had had to undergo such hardship. Her strength came from God and this sufficed for every day of her life.

Today is Reformation Sunday. In all Lutheran churches around the world, we are singing 'A mighty fortress is our God', a hymn written by Martin Luther, the five hundredth anniversary of whose birth we celebrate this year.[8]

Judgement—of God and Man
In concluding the story of Pastor Harri Mõtsnik, we find tragedy and hope in sharp juxtaposition. In 'Justice and Judgement' he reflects on his own calling as a pastor and in doing so he focusses on the ultimate question: the Last Judgement.

I have been asked why I am a pastor. My occupation and way of life were a mystery to my interlocutor. I answered: 'For no other reason than the salvation of your soul' ...

Death is the wages of sin and we cannot avoid the judgement of God. We will surely appear before his tribune and shall have to answer the question, 'What have you done to the least of your brethren' ... If not earlier, then at the last breath we shall experience the heart-rending question: 'What has been my relationship with God and my neighbour?' With death God's net is drawn up on the shores of eternity and then the sorting of the fish will take place, the separation of the worthy from the unworthy. God has put His hand on some already; they realise that they lack Him. The net has been drawn on the shore in their lives already; the sorting of the fish has begun.[9]

Judgement is of God and of God alone. It is too easy for Christians outside the Communist system to look at what must be an imperfect picture of religious life in the Soviet Union and pass judgement on those who have to live entirely within that system. One is asked, *ad nauseam*, to comment upon the motivation of the leaders of the registered churchs. 'Are they KGB agents?' is the usual question. Then of the leaders of the unregistered churches, the question comes, 'Aren't they just trouble makers? Don't they have a martyr complex?' Though Harri Mõtsnik preached his sermons in a registered church, the latter questions will undoubtedly be asked of him. It is better that such questions should not be formulated, let alone answered, by someone who is far removed from the scene. We must set out the facts insofar as they are known and leave them to speak for themselves.

Given the prevailing conditions in the Soviet Union—the continuing, unremitting, physical as well as psychological struggle against religion—not to mention the special shock which the authorities must have experienced to see such a religious revival with such intensive focus in an area where they had some ground for believing that the propaganda of a dying church was actually true—it was inevitable that Harri Mõtsnik would not be allowed to continue his ministry. Had his sermons been in the Russian language, it is doubtful whether so many of them would have been preached over a period of more than three years. The KGB network is not quite well enough organised to pick up 'subversion' in the Estonian language, which remains a dense mystery to those who were not brought up to speak it.

Pastor Mõtsnik's action in sending abroad a collection of his sermons sharpened the coming conflict, but was not the cause of it, for it was already inevitable. During the last year of his incumbency (1984) the journal of the Estonian Evangelical Lutheran Church in exile in Sweden published 13 sermons at his own request. It may well be that he felt this to be his only possible defence, since his ministry was already doomed. More is the pity, therefore, that these sermons remained locked in the Estonian language for two years, by which time the tragedy had passed its climax.

From every Christan and moral standpoint, Pastor Mõtsnik was justified in acting as he did. Had he been black and expressing the same kind of sentiments on 'liberation' in South Africa, he would long since have become a world hero and a household name. But part of the tragedy of the outspoken Christian in the Soviet Union who knows no fear is that he must remain almost totally isolated from the support of world public opinion. It is difficult enough to rouse even as much public support within the country as Harri Mõtsnik did, and even when this happens it is inevitable that there will be sharp criticism from the top leadership of the registered denomination itself.

Faced with an opponent who was totally unmindful of his personal safety, who was in the top educational bracket and who actually had a platform, however restricted, from which to speak, the KGB clearly deliberated for long over what tactics to adopt. Removal from Urvaste, arrest and trial on grounds of anti-Soviet activity in the form of fomenting nationalism would be only too easy. There were people in prison at that very time for the same offence and hundreds had been found guilty of it over the 40 years since the incorporation of Estonia into the Soviet Union. There would be difficulties, however. The public platform of a registered pulpit, around which people had been regularly gathering in their hundreds, had made Pastor Mõtsnik far better known among Estonians than those whose 'public' activities had necessarily been restricted to the circulation of clandestine documents. A trial risked instigating a demonstration, not a pleasing prospect for the KGB in a republic which had long since appeared, at least to outsiders, 'pacified'. Then the judicial training, the formidable logic and the very vibration of the voice itself in what to him were the familiar surroundings of a court of law: these factors combined to make him an opponent not to be taken on lightly, even where every card could be stacked against him.

In such circumstances, incarceration in a penal mental institution would have been the first possible course of action. It had been used many times before, with relative success, except that the victim would become yet another 'martyr'. Whole books have been published in the West about this specific tactic and its implementation proved many times over. The focus of protest would be uncomfortably close: a Lutheran victim would arouse Lutheran public opinion in the countries where that church predominated, most especially Sweden, but, even more uncomfortably, in neighbouring Finland. And it is a fact that public opinion was stirred in those countries while Mõtsnik was not even a name on a list elsewhere.

That they still went ahead with a trial indicates that the KGB felt it had already broken its man and that his 'confession' would follow shortly. In the case of Father Dimitri Dudko (Chapter 10), the confession obviated the need for any trial at all. Here it followed soon after.

The intimidation by the KGB had already begun, as we

have seen, in Leningrad, but this only compounded the problem by driving Pastor Mõtsnik back to his homeland, where his ministry immediately became more effective. Now came direct intervention by the KGB, with interrogation in the hostile surroundings of their offices. As we have seen, Pastor Mõtsnik, after release from one such session in the autumn of 1983, noted down some of the key points and sent them for publication as a postscript to *What Is Needed for Peace?*

After interrogation about his public reference to the 1983 destruction of the Korean airliner, during which he defended himself vigorously, on the grounds that this was an urgent matter in the discussion of the peace issue which was so central to the concerns of the Soviet churches, he stated that other violations were massively worse than this. The official warning was uncompromising: further such sermons would lead to his inevitable dismissal from his parish.

We can only guess at the pressure which built up before that final sermon, preaching after which he attempted to find peace in his native countryside. The process of breaking him was obviously a long one, involving not only the KGB interrogations, but also intimidation of his estranged wife, and doubtless his children. She was arrested in Tallinn on the same day, 3rd April 1985, along with many of his other associates. Their release followed after lengthy interrogation.

Possibly the most severe pressure of all came from his own church leaders. Archbishop Edgar Hark of Tallinn described him as 'a man with whom we could not cooperate', who refused to stop his 'system-criticising activities' even after repeated warnings. The KGB spread two rumours to undermine his support: firstly, that early release was planned if there was no outcry about his arrest; and secondly that he was an agent provocateur set to bring latent opposition among young pastors out in the open.

The trial, illegally secret, took place on 4–5th October

1985. It seems from the scrappy evidence that Pastor Mõtsnik could not call all the defence witnesses he wished, and that public access was limited to a few with no religious affiliations, given time off from work in order to foment a hostile atmosphere.

The accused admitted that he had written certain texts which he had passed to foreigners, that he had listened to foreign radio broadcasts and tape-recorded some of them referring to himself, including readings of his sermons, and he had circulated such tapes. He went on to affirm that he still believed in what he had done, even after interrogation in prison over the last six months. His sentence was three years in a labour camp. But he never left Tallinn, presumably to make it easier for his interrogators to break him in isolation and prevent other prisoners from finding out what was going on.

Just under six months later he walked out a free, but apparently broken man. What had happened? His treatment had clearly been so harsh as to cause a major breakdown in his health, a combination of tuberculosis, gastric ulcer (which was operated on) and heart palpitations.[10] The state apparatus was terrified and galvanized into action by one solitary preacher who had no weapon but his voice.

Very soon after his imprisonment a series of indications began to appear that he had 'confessed' or 'renounced his activities'. It is very hard to ascertain exactly what he meant to say to the world at this point. Statements from prison camp relayed by Soviet newspaper reporters (in early December) are clearly suspect; there was a TV appearance on 4th January 1986, of which no text is available, and it is not even possible to judge how genuine is his own 'signed' confession which appeared on 19th February 1986 in the Russian-language newspaper, *Soviet Estonia*. Did he actually write it? Was he forced to sign someone else's text—or did he actually sign it at all?

It is very probable that he did have a good deal to do with the text, because, upon analysis, it is obvious that the authorities did not extract from him quite such a breast-beating confession as they had hoped. Pastor Mõtsnik began by noting his sentence and his background, including the information, so interesting for a Soviet reader, that he had gone on to theological study after a career in law. He came into contact while in Leningrad with various foreigners (all the names are Scandinavian) who 'kindly offered to help the young people in my parish'. A correspondence began, but the pastor did not realise how what he wrote could be used 'against me and our state'. But, when passed on, these materials were used 'in a dishonourable and cruel way' by Estonian émigrés and foreign radio broadcasts. This activity continued after his move back to Estonia, even though he was by now in a depressed state owing to 'discord which had arisen in my parish at Pushkin, my relations with the Consistory (central church administration), the death of my parents and disagreement within my family'. He concluded by saying that he fully realised that his activities had been directed against the Soviet state and his extreme and baseless conclusions did not reflect the 'objective situation'. Writing offended letters to the Consistory and considering himself alone to be 'on the right path' was a delusion. 'I have fully admitted my guilt and condemn my previous activity.'[11]

These words secured his release on 28th March 1986, but they are some way from being a categorical denial of the truth of what he wrote. Rather, they throw the emphasis on the 'misuse' of this information abroad and on his personal difficulties (the mention of the death of his parents, who must have been in their eighties, illustrates just how thin the arguments are).

Even if Pastor Mõtsnik had renounced his faith (which he did not even come close to doing), even if he had denied the truth of everything which he said in his sermons, they are on the record, not only in the West, but more importantly in the hearts and minds of those who heard them. The religious revival in which he has played such an outstanding role cannot be inhibited by his recantation. The consequences of his bravery for future direct growth remain in place. As he himself says, coming up to retirement age, he now expects to pass on the baton to the younger generation and the future is in their hands. The same is true of Christian congregations all over the Soviet Union. Young people are rising to the challenge.

Chapter 3

Siberian Pentecostals: Resistance under Pressure

In the summer of 1981 the tiny Eastern Siberian settlement of Chuguyevka near the Pacific coast, about 6,000 miles east of Moscow, received an influx of settlers from another part of the Soviet Union. Their home town was Akhangaran in Uzbekistan, a Muslim-dominated area of Soviet Central Asia which could hardly have been more different, in terms of its geographical features, climate, local culture and traditions, from the inhospitable but beautiful expanses of Siberia.

They came in groups, several families a week until there were over 200 of them. A close-knit community who did not readily mix, their ethnic origins were German and they still spoke the language. They were poor and could not afford to buy homes. Having little in the way of material possessions, they set to work to build simple timber houses.

The locals noticed immediately that this group not only shared their possessions with each other, but their time and talents too. Everyone helped with the building work, providing first for the families with the largest number of children and dependent elderly relatives (some of them numbered 12 or more). The men, mainly skilled or semi-skilled workers, found employment in local industrial plants and factories. They quickly earned a reputation for being diligent and conscientious, seemingly an asset to the local community. So it must have been a shock, at least to some of the ordinary Chuguyevka townspeople, when soon after their arrival the local Communist authorities branded the newcomers as criminals, ripe for humiliation and persecution.

Unfortunately, Chuguyevka did not differ from Akhangaran in the one essential for which this community had hoped: freedom to practise their faith as Pentecostals and to bring up their children as Christians. The indignities which they suffered at the hands of the local and regional authorities were eventually to lead to a show of strength, courage and integrity which deserves to be brought to the attention of the worldwide Christian public. Apart from recording their own story in a series of letters and documents somehow sent out of the Soviet Union, this community has given us a remarkable glimpse of its life in an amateur cinefilm.

It is not absolutely clear why they decided to leave Akhangaran or why they chose Eastern Siberia as their destination, although it is known that some of the families concerned had lived in this region of the USSR before. One possibility is that they hoped to find better employment prospects. They may also have feared that sooner or later active measures would be taken against them because of their Christian activities and decided to move before this came about. It *is* certain that they were unanimous in their decision and over a period of about a year the whole religious community resettled.

Origins

The Pentecostal movement began in Russia just before the Revolution and grew considerably in the 1920s. It was also strong in the Baltic Republics, Eastern Poland and other areas incorporated into the USSR during World War II.

The Chuguyevka Pentecostals are no fanatics. They are mainstream Pentecostals belonging to the movement founded by Ivan Voronaev. He left Russia before the Revolution as a Baptist and lived in the USA, where he became a Pentecostal. He returned to the USSR in 1920, sponsored by the Assemblies of God in America, to spread Pentecostalism in his homeland. He was arrested twice and served terms in labour camp and exile. Most of his children emigrated from the Soviet Union while he was in prison. After his first sentence, he too tried to obtain permission to re-emigrate to the USA, but he was re-arrested and never heard of again. His wife also spent some time in prison, but was eventually allowed to emigrate to the USA in 1964, where she died.

Most Pentecostals called themselves 'Christians of evangelical faith'. Within the USSR they shared in the general suffering of the 1930s, but in August 1945 the authorities offered them legality if they merged with the Evangelical Christians and Baptists (ECB). This has proved unacceptable for many Pentecostals, who either refused to join the Baptists or subsequently withdrew from the Union.

There is no reason, other than Soviet intimidation, why Pentecostals should be expected to become Baptists (the effect of the 1945 agreement) in order to live legally as Christians under the system. The issue of registration by the state was for them an acute one, being tantamount to agreeing to lose their identity, though many would have been prepared to register as Pentecostals if the system had permitted it.

Those who resisted assimilation made themselves liable to especially systematic persecution, particularly because of their steadfast determination to bring up their children in their own faith. The resistance, too, has had a quality of steel and much of this has become well known through the documents the Pentecostals have sent out; from the 'invasion' of the American Embassy by Siberian Pentecostals in 1963, from Pastor Fedotov's congregation at Kaluga in 1974, from the 'Siberian Seven' (inside the American Embassy for five years after 1978) and several other instances.

A New Campaign

The small community in Chuguyevka has now become one of the best documented. The situation there has remained unchanged in its essentials since the Soviet authorities first took stock of their activities. In June 1981 Viktor Walter, the pastor, received an official warning:

> You have not responded to numerous warnings by representatives of the local authorities about violations by your religious society of the Legislation on Religious Cults and their proposals that you should legalise the society by registration. Instead you are continuing to conduct illegal and anti-social activities. In accordance with Article 4 of the Decree on Religious Associations you are instructed to terminate any organised religious activity of the society until it is registered in accordance with the law. Otherwise you personally will be held responsible in accordance with the law.[1]

Pastor Walter must have felt a deep sense of foreboding when he received this warning. It was the first unmistakable sign that he and his congregation were not welcome in Chuguyevka, at least by the Communists.

Viktor, however, is a man of strong will and character who has not had an easy life and has learned to accept many trials and difficulties. Born in 1950, he was one of ten children and had to leave school at the age of 16 in order to find work and help support the family. He became a Christian at the age of 18. He served in the Soviet Army, but refused to swear the military oath because of his Christian convictions. That would have been the first really difficult test for him in his Christian life. He was married in 1975 in Akhangaran, where he and his young wife, Masha, made their first home and where he became pastor of the local Pentecostal congregation.

After the move to Chuguyevka and a period of settling in, Viktor resumed his responsibility for organising the spiritual life of the community. They had never known what it was to have a church building so they simply continued their practice of meeting for worship in each others' homes. Their services are unstructured and informal, with a great emphasis on singing and open prayer. Guitars and accordions are used for accompaniment. The time of worship often concluded with a communal meal, pictured in their home movie.

The local authorities infiltrated the meetings to write down the names of all those present. The message from the authorities was now 'Register or else...' Valeri Chupin, a Government official from Vladivostok, gave them a booklet, *Religion and the Law*, explaining the conditions of registration.

There had been a modification of Soviet policy over the last decade (the 'merge under threat' policy having failed). Some Pentecostal registrations were now permitted.

No legal advice being available to the community, the whole church discussed the issue and unanimously concluded that the law on registration was contrary to the teaching of the Bible and to many of God's commandments; to comply with it would amount to a renunciation of the truth. One unacceptable condition, among others, would have been to renounce religious education for the children.

On 15th June 1981 Viktor Walter and a member of the congregation, Anatoli Khokha, were summoned by the authorities. They fined Viktor 50 roubles (approximately one-third of the average monthly wage for a manual labourer) and threatened Anatoli, who had been host to the Sunday services, to comply with the law on registration. Now the campaign against them began in earnest.

On 30th August 1981 local officials interrupted the Sunday morning service and took down the names of all those present. Further fines followed. On 30th October all the Pentecostals were notified about a compulsory meeting to be held at the House of Culture. They arrived to find Valeri Chupin in the chair, with a crowd present obviously under instruction to create a hostile atmosphere.

Chupin adopted a relatively moderate tone initially, insisting that the Pentecostals should register their congregation. But as soon as they began to speak up for themselves and explain the reason why, for conscience sake, they could not register, Chupin became angry. He began to slander the believers and incite the gathering against them. Turning to the whole assembly he announced, 'If they will not register voluntarily, we will hound them until they do.' The believers were given ten days to reach a decision.

Far from being intimidated by these threats, the Pentecostals were more determined than ever not to give in and thereby, as they saw it, lose their integrity.

They continued to worship together despite the ten-day warning. On 15th November officials burst into the Sunday morning service and demanded that it should stop. The believers carried on regardless, praying all the while for their persecutors. At the end, Christian Stumpf, who owned the house where they were gathered that day, and fellow-believer, Yegor Betkher, were taken away in a black maria and locked in a cell. On the following day both men were given 15 days' detention (a summary punishment commonly given under the Soviet system). On 17th November Elvira, Christian's daughter, was sentenced to two months 'corrective labour' with a loss of 20 per cent of her wages because she had recited poetry at a service of worship (another common punishment, involving assignment to a particular job and loss of earnings).

On the following Sunday the service took place in the home of Wilhelm Rosher. This time believers present took photographs as the interruption occurred. As soon as they realised what was happening, the militia tried to snatch the cameras, but the photographers managed to get away. As a result the militia called at all the believers' homes that evening in an attempt to find the guilty photographers. By nightfall two more members of the church had been arrested. The militia tried to force them to hand over their cameras and film (now hidden), but they categorically refused. The next day there was a summary trial of the five. Two were sentenced to ten days' detention.

Two weeks later Leonard Voitke's house was the scene of the service, when it was again disrupted. Since the photograph incident the militia had decided to use an ordinary civilian car. This time they simply picked out various individuals and issued them with a summons after the service. As a result, six believers were punished with either fines or detentions on the next day. Samuel Walter, Viktor's father, was fined a total of 100 roubles. His income as a pensioner was only 120 roubles a month, on which he had to support a dependent son who was not earning while he was a student, so in a single day he became destitute.

The consequences of the punishments meted out on that occasion were most serious for Gennadi Maidanyuk. After serving ten days in detention he returned to work. His boss angrily demanded to know where he had been. Gennadi replied that he had been given a ten-day sentence for reading the Bible at a service of worship. He was instantly demoted from bus driver to stoker with consequent reduction of earnings.

Meanwhile the authorities stepped up the pressure, now disrupting week-day meetings as well. Every Wednesday and Friday they visited believers' homes at random, peering through windows and demanding to know where the evening meeting would be held. The usual reprisals followed—arrests, fines, detentions, corrective labour and loss of wages. The large Pentecostal families were now in serious financial difficulties and they decided collectively to appeal to the authorities in the regional centre, Vladivostok.

A delegation consisting of Viktor and Samuel Walter and Christian Stumpf travelled there on 23rd December. Chupin and others received them. They handed over a document stating that between them they had had to pay over 1,500 roubles in fines in the last month. They were promised immediate investigation of their complaints.

It is understandable that a group living in a perpetual crisis should tell us more of their external struggle than their inner spiritual state. However, it is clear that their steadfastness and calm impressed members of the local community. People began to take a closer interest in their affairs to see what would happen next and many of them, far from being hostile to the believers, abhorred the unjust and brutal actions of the militia and the KGB.

An article in the local newspaper provides clear evidence that, despite the many difficulties they faced as a congregation, the Pentecostals were actively witnessing to non-believers.[2] The author describes how, in 1982, Tanya Walter, Viktor's niece, talked of her faith to her school friends. The parents were doubtless doing the same at their places of work and in their contacts with local people.

One of the aims of the article is to demonstrate the inadequacy and irresponsibility of Christian parents who, by bringing up their children to believe in God, deny them the joys of childhood and turn them into fanatics. For example, the author reveals that the children from Pentecostal families who joined the school in 1982 avoided contact with fellow-pupils and immediately felt themselves to be outsiders because their parents forbade them to go to the cinema, read books or watch television. Allegedly such activities were 'against God'. At the same time, the author reveals that Tanya Walter was telling her friends about Christ:

But Tanya, the most forward one, immediately made friends with her neighbour, Marina Shkriyabina, and explained to her secretly, 'Those who believe in God receive spiritual gifts; they receive the Holy Spirit. But the sinful world separates man from God.' And in order to affirm these words she surreptitiously showed her friend some Christian literature under the cover of her desk lid.[3]

1982 saw further repression. The chief of militia, Major Dobysh, told Viktor Walter and Nikolai Stumpf in January that the commission completely upheld the local authorities and the campaign would now intensify. Viktor replied defiantly that he would write to the authorities in Moscow, for which they gave him ten days' detention.

As the situation worsened the believers began to keep a detailed record of the persecution. They sent a signed document to Leonid Brezhnev. There was no reply from Moscow. The matter was simply referred back to Vladivostok and the repression continued unchanged. The believers continued to hold their meetings, but exercised more caution. They varied the times of the services and gathered either in the early morning or late evening. They could no longer afford the risk of being discovered because they simply had no money to pay the fines. Some of them were forced to find extra work during their statutory holiday in order to feed their families.

In January 1983 five members of the congregation were warned that their children would be taken away from them if they continued to educate them 'in a religious spirit' at variance with state atheist education. The local education chief, Viktor Romanov, told believers that atheist indoctrination was an intrinsic part of state education. Four of the five parents were fined 50 roubles each for allowing their children to attend religious services. These fines were then repeated at the end of January. One of the parents, Anatoli Khokha, had nine to feed, apart from himself and his wife. He informed Romanov that he would be forced to look for a second job in order to earn enough money to pay the fine. He was promptly told that the authorities would make sure that he did not find any additional work.

In the Soviet Union it is unthinkable that a teacher who is responsible for educating a new generation of Soviet citizens 'in the spirit of Communism' should have sympathy with any religion. In order to qualify to teach even the tiniest infants, she (the vast majority are female) will have had to pass exams in scientific atheism. When called upon to deal with children who are believers or from Christian homes, the teachers, if they are career-minded, cannot afford to have any scruples when carrying out the instructions issued by the party organisations. This does not mean that humanitarian instincts and a sense of decency do not dictate against deliberate discrimination against believers' children. Very often teachers simply salve their consciences by passing the blame and responsibility on to the parents.[4]

Some accounts of the victimisation of Christian children, not just Pentecostals, are very disturbing. One's reaction is often incredulity at the unwillingness of parents to compromise a little for the sake of their children. But these sentiments are at variance with the philosophy of Christian fundamentalists who firmly believe that to make one gesture of compromise is to embark on a downward spiral. They would argue that, despite the suffering that some children have to endure at an early age when they cannot fully understand the issues involved for themselves, it produces in them a strength of character which stands them in good stead as Christians for the rest of their lives. There are many inspiring examples of the bravery and maturity of such children. However, there must be an equal number of untold stories of children who, at an early age, have been damaged psychologically because of persecution at school, and have had to live with the consequences for the rest of their lives. Perhaps it has caused some of them to reject the faith altogether.

During the first half of 1983 when mothers were under pressure because of fears for their children, the men were having difficulties at their places of work. Atheist lectures were organised specifically to incite hatred towards believers.

Similarly, during atheist lectures held for adults in the local school, believers had to listen to accusations that Christians were enemies of the state; their refusal to undertake military service proved it. A more chilling accusation, resurrected from the time of Stalin's excesses, was that Pentecostals slew children as human sacrifices. This slander campaign instigated a spate of attacks on believers' homes. Windows were smashed, clean laundry slashed and torn from washing lines to be trampled in the dirt. The authorities disassociated themselves entirely from these acts of vandalism, claiming that the believers themselves had perpetrated them.

To what extent such incidents were inspired by the hatred stirred up among the local population, which undoubtedly fuelled the desire of criminal elements to cause trouble, and to what extent they were actually orchestrated by the local authorities—is difficult to judge. If the latter had been successful in their efforts to incite antagonistic feelings against the believers, they would not have needed to employ resources and manpower patrolling the streets simply to find out where Pentecostal meetings were being held. The neighbours could easily have informed on them, but there is no indication that they did so. At the same time, fear prevents ordinary people from openly defending victimised believers.

One Sunday in February 1983 a group of believers planned to go into the forest to collect firewood. They had obtained the necessary permit in advance, both to collect the wood and to use a log transporter. Vladimir Walter, who worked as a crane operator, received a permit to use the crane for a few hours for loading the firewood into the log transporter.

On the same day the militia carried out an especially intensive search, hoping to find the venue for the morning service. From 7am cordons consisting of schoolchildren and Komsomol (Young Communist League) members were stationed outside nearly all the believers' homes, and several militia vehicles cruised around the streets. These cars followed the believers as they emerged from their homes, including those going to the forest to collect wood. As a result, the militia stopped the crane and prevented the men from continuing. They confronted Vladimir Walter with an accusation. On the following day he explained precisely what had happened to the administration at his firm. But his boss and the mechanic who had issued him with the permit appeared to be unconcerned. A commission met to discuss the incident on 22nd February and subsequently Vladimir's driving licence was revoked for one year, thus depriving him of his means of earning a living. He had to support his wife and eight small children. Even some members of the commission protested against the harshness of this punishment and said he was innocent.

This incident again illustrates the fact that there were people who were convinced of the integrity of the Pentecostal community and who were prepared to speak out against injustice, despite intimidation by the authorities.

In one of their documents the Pentecostals summed up all these events as follows:

Everything that we have described here in this document—and the militia admitted this on more than one occasion—was ordered from 'on high'. Some of the believers asked the chief of militia, Dobysh, when this reign of terror would cease. He replied calmly, 'We are soldiers. We deal with you according to our orders and if we are ordered not to persecute you we shall stop.'[5]

The Attempt to Emigrate
However, the soldiers continued to receive their orders. The Chuguyevka Pentecostals decided they could no longer endure the conditions in which they were being forced to live and a large number decided to apply for emigration to West Germany. On 30th March 1983 50 believers sent their passports, together with a declaration renouncing

their Soviet citizenship and a request for permission to emigrate to West Germany, to the Presidium of the Supreme Soviet of the USSR. At the beginning of April they notified the regional authorities in Vladivostok about their action. It would be four months before they received an official reply—a refusal—and in the intervening period the campaign against them intensified. Several articles appeared in the local newspaper portraying them as extremists and even spies. Teachers again made life very difficult for believers' children. They depicted life in West Germany as wretched. They introduced more atheist propaganda into their lessons with the aim of deliberately insulting believers' children. The teachers portrayed these children as misguided and ignorant and their parents as evil fanatics. After the refusal of the children to attend an insulting atheist film, teachers incited other children to beat them up and call them names. They arrived home bruised, bloodstained and in tears, but despite numerous appeals no redress followed.

In June, representatives from the visa office in Vladivostok arrived in Chuguyevka and invited all those who had surrendered their passports to discuss the matter. They exerted great pressure on them to reclaim their passports which had been returned from Moscow. None of the believers would agree to do so. They were subsequently threatened and bullied and told they would never be permitted to leave the Soviet Union. Colonel Spirin from the visa office mocked them, saying they would all end up with their 'heads in a noose'. When the Pentecostals reminded him about their constitutional rights, he told them: 'The laws are not for the likes of you; there are no laws for you'.[6] Before he left, Colonel Spirin instructed the local authorities to penalise those who were living without their internal passports. In the summer three mothers gave birth and the local registry office refused to issue birth certificates until the parent produced their internal passports to prove their identity.

Now a new phase began. After they had received official refusal of permission to emigrate, 70 believers declared a hunger strike of up to ten days from 5th September, the first of a series which continued into 1986. Of the 70 members of the congregation who participated in the hunger strike, 20 were children aged 7 to 11 years who fasted for 24 hours. Sixteen pregnant women and nursing mothers fasted for three days, 11 other women for five days and 23 men for ten days. A commission arrived again from Vladivostok and they angrily insisted that the Pentecostals reclaim their passports. The believers declared in response that if there were no satisfactory outcome after the hunger strike, they would declare another one.

Their action was ignored, so they wrote to the authorities announcing a month-long hunger strike to begin on 12th January 1984. They planned this in as much detail as the first, assessing everyone's capacity to undertake the action. They also sent an open letter to the West German and Soviet governments, the UN General Assembly and world media, announcing their plan to renew the hunger strike and insisting on their right to emigrate in accordance with all Soviet and international laws.

Following this decisive action there was a glimmer of hope. For the first time the authorities became defensive. They obviously felt that a major scandal was in the making and decided to stall for time and reclaim the initiative.

On 23rd December 1983 Viktor Walter, together with 20 other men from the congregation, attended a meeting with government officials. A lengthy discussion took place. They were informed that, starting before March, they would be allowed to emigrate to West Germany, providing they had bona-fide invitations from relatives there, but that they could not go in large groups. The men decided to test the possibility of a peaceful departure and postponed the second hunger strike. However, the authorities did not keep their word.

In response, the church members again sent in their in-

ternal passports and they organised a 20-day hunger strike
to commence on 15th September 1984. As a result, all the
participants lost their jobs.

A Cine-Film

It is at this point in their story that we can observe these
heroic people in detail on the cine-film referred to earlier
which somehow reached the West.

It shows a group of about 20 men assembled in a house
and huddled together for warmth. A poster on the wall
indicates that this is day 30, the last day of the second
hunger strike. Another section of film, shot later, shows a
poster attached to the outside of one of the believers'
houses with the text: 'In this house a third hunger strike is
taking place as a sign of protest to the Presidium of the Supreme Soviet of the USSR. Allow us to emigrate to West
Germany. Day 11.' Then the police remove the poster.

Next we see day 22 of the third hunger strike. The police
again arrive at Anatoli Khokha's house to remove the
offending poster. But they discover after removing it that
the text has actually been stencilled on to the wall of the
house. On day 23 we see the militia obliterating the stencilled text with tar.

Apart from the groups of militia shown on the film who
appear to go about their duty with resignation rather than
with great relish, there are shots of curious onlookers. This
public attention must have strengthened the resolve of the
local authorities to bring the whole embarrassing episode to
a speedy conclusion.

The most poignant section of the film shows another
event which took place just a week after the end of the
second hunger strike—the funeral of Samuel Walter. He
had gone into hospital for a minor operation during the
second week in October and was recovering well, when he
was suddenly moved into a side ward and his family were
refused access to him. Within 24 hours he was dead. The

diagnosis on the death certificate was lung cancer. Samuel's family were extremely suspicious about the circumstances in which he died, claiming that he had never, to their knowledge, had any chest problems in his life and had been in excellent general health prior to the operation. They also claimed that the KGB had spoken to the doctors at the hospital. Being keen amateur photographers, they happened to have filmed Samuel a few weeks before his death looking after his bees in the countryside. Far from having the appearance of a man dying from cancer, he looks a picture of health.

The funeral took place on 21 October in a blizzard. The film shows the funeral procession through the village on foot with members of the family carrying the open coffin (Evangelicals follow Russian Orthodox custom in this funeral practice). The route followed by the mourners was later to become a matter of dispute with the authorities, who claimed Viktor Walter had not obtained the necessary permission to use that particular route. The faithful loaded the coffin on to a lorry, which went to the cemetery. There is a very moving scene showing members of the family and the congregation at the graveside paying their last respects. Snow is carefully wiped away from Samuel's face as the mourners kiss his forehead in a final farewell before the coffin is sealed and lowered into the grave.

Some time later the believers erected a beautiful, hand-crafted headstone at the graveside to commemorate the life and death of Samuel Walter and another Pentecostal believer. It bears their photographs and the inscription 'Here are buried Christian believers,' with details about their lives. Believers gently lower the headstone on to a horse-drawn cart and take it to the cemetery, where there is a pause for a prayer of dedication.

Despite the poor quality of the film, the scenes portrayed, several of which have now been seen on British television, leave a lasting impression of the dignity and devotion with which these believers mark the most solemn moments of their lives. The funeral procession through the town is an act of Christian witness to the whole community. The more intimate gathering at the graveside provides an opportunity for the whole church, including the children, to honour the memory of the departed, to share the family's grief and to console each other with Christian hope.

In November 1984 an article appeared in the local newspaper reproaching the Pentecostals who wished to leave the Soviet Union for making use of 'rights and privileges'.[7] They were criticised for having received free state education for themselves and their children and for receiving free medical treatment. The believers knew that schoolchildren would pick up these latest accusations from the press and use them as a basis for further taunts at school. Eight sets of parents took the drastic step of withdrawing their children from school from 29th November. They sent a signed declaration announcing their decision to the national and regional authorities.

Seven days later all the parents were summoned to the authorities, but as they had already been on hunger strike for 22 days (since 14 November) they were too weak to attend, with the exception of Vladimir Walter who represented them all. The message was clear—fines and the threat of putting the children into care. All the children must attend school the next day. The Regional Procurator knew that all the parents concerned had lost their jobs as a result of the September-October hunger strike and they would therefore be unable to pay the fines, so he informed Vladimir that the Procuracy had the right to confiscate possessions to the value of 30 roubles instead.

On the same day, in the evening, the Procurator, accompanied by militia, called at the home of Viktor Walter to read an official statement indicating that unless Viktor and members of his congregation complied with certain conditions there would be legal proceedings against him and all other members of the congregation. No further services of worship were to be held without the registration of the congregation. Believers' passports were to be redeemed and the children sent back to school. On 9th December the Sunday service at Valeri Lobzov's house was interrupted. Those present were photographed. Following this, the authorities spread the rumour that the Pentecostals were not on hunger strike at all. By the 25th day many of the participants were feeling extremely weak. Viktor Walter had lost 18 kilos. Between the second and third hunger strikes there had been an interval of just one month, barely enough time for them to recover physically.

The next move on the part of the authorities was to carry out a series of house searches in 15 homes. They confiscated religious literature, Bibles, psalters, children's poetry books, addresses, letters and photographs. They behaved particularly brutally in the homes of Viktor Walter, Valeri Lobzov and Anatoli Khokha. In Viktor's house they attempted to take up the floor and dismantle the ceiling. Valeri Lobzov tried to cling on to his Bible, his most treasured possession, but the KGB wrenched his arms back and grabbed it from him. His wife, Evgenia, was given a body-search in front of her nine terrified children. Anatoli was feeling ill when the KGB arrived. Before the end of the search they announced that he was under arrest. He was about to say goodbye to the family, but suddenly fainted. Despite this, he was brutally manhandled and thrust into a waiting car.

The searches lasted six hours and at the end Viktor Walter and Nikolai Vins were arrested in addition to Anatoli, although the former were released four days later. When Viktor stepped outside his house, it was surrounded by militia who prevented anyone from approaching him to say goodbye. For many this was the last glimpse they would have of their pastor for a long time. Some of the relatives went by car to the police station to find out where they were taking him. They were informed that he was already being escorted to Vladivostok, a journey of about 200 miles.

He was charged under six articles of the RSFSR Criminal

Code, and the trial took place in April 1985. Under article 142 ('violation of the laws on the separation of church and state') he was charged with refusing to register the church and organising the funeral of his father. Under article 227 ('infringement of the person and rights of citizens under the guise of performing religious rituals') he was charged with organising the hunger strikes conducted by the church, thereby damaging the health of the participants, refusing medical treatment and organising meetings for children and young people. Under article 190–3 ('organising group activities which disrupt public order') he was charged with organising the hunger strikes and the display of posters announcing them. He was also accused in court of creating a public nuisance by singing hymns and reading psalms during his father's funeral procession.

During his final address to the court, Viktor stated that he considered it a great honour to be entrusted with the pastoral oversight of the church. His sentence was five years, for which he has been transferred to a labour camp 3,700 miles away at Velsk, near Arkhangelsk, in the polar region of European Russia, since when his family have twice been refused permission to visit him.

Shortly after Viktor's arrest in December 1984, 20 members of the congregation took part in a public demonstration demanding the release of their pastor. Seven of them were later tried and sentenced for this. Those Pentecostals who remain at liberty have done their best to defend these victims, staging further hunger strikes and appealing to world leaders, but so far without any response.

In February 1986 Keston College received information that the situation of the Pentecostals in Chuguyevka had become even more difficult. One of the greatest problems was food: they had already killed and eaten all the animals they owned and were surviving on ten roubles a month for an adult and five roubles for a child. Parcels have been sent from the West, but they cannot claim them because they neither have passports for identification, nor money to pay the duty.

For the families of the imprisoned members of the
church, the well-being of their relatives is naturally a matter
of constant concern. According to information received at
Keston College, only one of the prisoners is being confined
in Chuguyevka itself, where there is an ordinary-regime
labour camp. The other prisoners have been sent to different locations to serve their sentences, almost all considerable distances from their home town. There is no shortage
of labour camps in the Pacific Maritime Province where
Chuguyevka is located and in the neighbouring
Khabarovsk Province, so the scattering of the prisoners
across the country appears to be a deliberate policy to make
a difficult situation even harder for the prisoners and their
families. Nikolai Vins, serving five years, is located even
further away from his family than Viktor Walter. He is
imprisoned in Krasnovodsk on the Eastern shore of the
Caspian Sea, over 4,000 miles from home.

There will doubtless be a further chapter to write about
this Pentecostal community and one prays that it will be a
less tragic one. It is inconceivable that the Chuguyevka
Pentecostals, having suffered so much already, will give up
their struggle now. The Apostle Paul described himself as
an 'ambassador in chains' (Eph 6:20). Viktor Walter and
the other imprisoned members of the Chuguyevka church
follow in a sacred tradition and they too are doubtless
shedding the light of the Gospel in places where there is a
desperate need. They themselves have experienced
spiritual growth; the community has maintained itself
against the full might of the state; children swell the numbers. It would not be surprising to see converts added to
their church.

Chapter 4

Central Asian Mennonites: Minority of a Minority

There are not many Protestants in Central Asia. Islam holds sway, despite unceasing Soviet efforts to diminish its influence. The Christian minority is mainly Orthodox, with a few groups of Protestants (chiefly Baptists). Yet a smaller minority of Protestants, German-speaking, like the Chuguyevka Pentecostals, clings tenaciously to its origins: Mennonites who refuse to be submerged in the seas around them.

For these tiny and scattered German-speaking communities, to speak Russian, let alone to adopt the atheist values of Soviet society, is to betray their origins. Yet there are some signs that their leaders are prepared to encourage the first, while resisting the second. A visitor in 1986, Peter Rempel, of the Mennonite Central Committee's European office, explains the possibilities and at the same time underlines the contradiction between persecution and tolerance of religion under the Soviet system.

The Mennonite churches are experiencing more freedom in the USSR than they have since the Revolution. This is a time of building churches, baptising new members and ordaining new ministers. It is a time of ordering congregational life and of attaining material well-being. It is a time of restoring contacts between the scattered fellowships in the USSR and the Mennonite fellowship abroad.[1]

A Brief History

Mennonites have arrived at this more hopeful point in Soviet history only after overcoming immense obstacles. They originated in both Switzerland and the Netherlands. The Swiss founder was a young patrician and scholar, Conrad Grebel (1498–1526), originally a follower of Zwingli, who in 1525 inaugurated believers' baptism and set up a free church. The members of the new church were nicknamed Anabaptists (rebaptisers). The movement spread rapidly, especially into Alsace and south Germany. Grebel's followers conceived of the church as a fellowship of converted people, baptised upon a commitment to Christ as Lord and maintaining strict discipline.

The group was characterised by the highest standards of morality because—they believed—their life of discipleship had to be evident for all to scrutinise. Their example involved the rejection of all oaths and of any form of military service. The Anabaptist movement was severely persecuted by both Catholic and Protestant states, but it continued to spread. The Mennonites took their name from Menno Simons, an early Dutch leader of the movement.

Mennonites first came to Russia from Prussia in 1788, during the reign of Catherine II who offered them a special colonisation agreement. This included, first and foremost, offers of land, but equally importantly a guarantee of self-administration, the right to preserve their own German language, freedom of religion, control of their own schools, exemption from military service and economic aid. The Mennonite colonists distinguished themselves as hardworking and thrifty, and they prospered. Initially they congregated in Southern Ukraine and along the Volga, but later they spread further east and settled in Western Siberia and Asiatic Russia.

At the time of the Russian Revolution of 1917 there were 120,000 Mennonites: 75,000 living in Ukraine, the others living in Siberia and other eastern areas. They suffered greatly during the ensuing civil war because they lived where fighting was fierce. Frequently bandits burned and looted their property, raping their wives and daughters. This led to the formation in the Mennonite community of an armed defence league and a temporary abandonment of their pacifist principles.

During the 1920s about 20,000 Mennonites emigrated to Canada and the United States. For those who remained in the Soviet Union, years of hardship were to follow. The enforced collectivisation of land during the first five-year plan (1928–32) shattered their tradition of careful individual husbandry. Many of them were forcibly resettled further east. Stalin's attack on religion, launched in 1929, brought an end to all organised religious life and resulted in numerous arrests of believers, among them many Mennonite church leaders.

In 1941 Hitler's armies invaded the Soviet Union and the Mennonite communities suffered physical and spiritual collapse. Stalin declared that all Germans in the USSR were actual or potential fifth-columnists and deported them *en masse* from European Russia. The men were separated from their wives and children and sent to work in labour colonies in the usual remote regions. Even their families were scattered in distant exile. Yet the women—and some men who survived—kept the faith alive.

A Wilderness Journey

A recent book, *A Wilderness Journey*, gives some moving first-hand accounts of the difficulties of those years.[2] The authors and compilers, father and son, Heinrich and Gerhard Woelk, served the Mennonite Brethren Church in

Karaganda in Kazakhstan for many years prior to their emigration to West Germany.

There is a passage by Mrs. Gertrude Tjahrt vividly depicting the horror and deprivation experienced by members of the Mennonite community as they were forced to abandon their homes and livelihood and journey into exile. She describes how they fled to the Caucasus in 1930 and lived there in fear for a whole decade. Then the Germans arrived and they escaped by train to the wilderness of Central Asia. Through all this they kept their faith alive.

The women met among themselves and took their children along, telling them Bible stories and singing gospel songs with them. In spite of the wretchedness of their banishment, they had managed to take along an occasional guitar, mandolin or old violin and some had taken parts of the 'Liederperlen' hymn book. So the mothers, who in their young years had sung or played in the choir, taught their children to use the instruments and sing the songs. There was a Tante Dickmann in the Kazakh village of Ulgi-Algan who knew almost all the Liederperlen songs and even their numbers.[3]

At the end of the war Stalin made a few concessions to the churches for their contribution to the war effort by permitting some of them to reopen, but this was controlled and selective. People were numbed by the devastation wrought by the war and their main preoccupation was simply finding enough food to eat in a country whose economy had to be rebuilt from top to bottom. As conditions gradually improved, people began to turn their attention to another type of hunger—spiritual hunger—and this resulted in a wave of revival. People began to gather together secretly for prayer and singing. Where a family had managed to retain a Bible, small groups met to read and meditate on it together.

In the mid-1950s a miracle happened. Some ministers imprisoned during the 1930s had completed their long camp

sentences or were amnestied after Stalin's death and returned to their families. Northern Kazakhstan and the city
of Karaganda attracted large numbers of Germans because
of the availability of jobs in the region's coal mines. Many
resumed their former preaching activity and became travel-
ling evangelists, conducting baptisms, organising churches
and ordaining ministers. A period of growth was experienced by other denominations. For many this resulted in
renewed prison terms or other forms of harassment after
the short-lived liberalisation. The period of renewal was
not without an accompanying sense of crisis. The believers
had virtually no tools for rebuilding their spiritual lives.
There were hardly any Bibles, let alone any other Christian
literature, no trained pastors or lay workers. Mrs Tjahrt, in
another account included in Heinrich Woelk's book, con-
veyed the atmosphere in the Mennonite community.

In 1950 some of the men who had been in banishment or in the
work brigades began to return. They saw the hunger for the Word
of God and felt this hunger themselves. Their first task they recognised as helping their women in this concern. Meetings were
arranged for Sundays and the Word of God was preached. This
had its effect and conversions followed. But nowhere in all these
villages was there an ordained minister. In the same year these
men gathered together (illegally) from all over the region in order
to find a way to carry on the work in the villages among the Germans who had been banished here. They agreed that everyone
would serve the spiritual needs of his own village and gather
groups for fellowship. The men took up this resolution with courage and joy. The young people and children were very receptive
to the Word of God, and many were converted. Meetings were
held in the most primitive of rooms; for benches, boards were supported by blocks of wood. Afterwards these had to be cleared
away. Groups formed to sing hymns, although the young people
were not familiar with four-part singing. Almost no song books
were available, so the older people had the responsibility of leading and teaching the singing.

The working day on the collective farms was in shifts from 5am until late at night.

The girls were mainly milkmaids, the boys worked with farm
machinery (tractors and combines). After a hard day's work, instead of going to bed, a horse and wagon would be taken and
driven to the next village, where a part of the night would be spent
singing and studying the Bible. That was indeed hunger for the
Word of God![4]

Mrs Tjahrt goes on to say that people assiduously copied
out by hand hymns and even whole devotional books. The
number of secret meetings grew, and there were many secret baptisms in rivers and lakes.

New Horizons

It was precisely this type of spiritual experience that was to
enrich the life of the Mennonite Brethren Church in
Karaganda that eventually came into being in 1956. Clearly
one of the reasons for its vitality today is the contribution
made to it in the early years by Mennonite families who had
learned how to depend on God entirely for their survival
during the years of separation and exile.

Before they obtained the concession of an indepen-
dently-registered Mennonite Brethren church, the Mennonite Brethren worshipped with the Karaganda Baptists.
Spiritual revival and hunger for God's word were growing.
Denominational affiliations were made insignificant, at
least temporarily. What united believers was the need to
share their faith in Christ in the face of a state hostile to all
religion.

However, there had been a notable split in the ranks of
the Mennonites in 1860, from which the New Mennonites
(Mennonite Brethren Church) as distinct from the Church
Mennonites ('Kirchliche') emerged. The fundamental disagreement between the two concerns the method of
baptism. The Mennonite Brethren adopted baptism by full
immersion from the Baptists. The Church Mennonites

practise baptism by sprinkling. These two distinct branches persist in the Soviet Union and elsewhere to this day.

Although the Baptist church in Karaganda was not directly persecuted, registration restricted its evangelistic preaching and its work with children. A grave disadvantage for the German members of the congregation was that the Russian language predominated, while German still had the tinge of being the language of the enemy. This caused some bitterness and gave rise to suspicion and mistrust on the part of some of the Russian Baptist church leaders.

In addition to attending services at the Baptist church, Mennonites met for fellowship whenever they dared in each others' homes. Such meetings were strictly forbidden, but they used the pretext of family gatherings such as birthdays to pray, sing and listen to readings from the Bible. Eventually, in 1956, 21 of the Mennonite Brethren and their families decided to withdraw completely from the Baptist Church in Karaganda, and they formed the nucleus of the Mennonite Brethren Church.[5] In the same year an elderly ordained minister, Dietrich Pauls (born 1886), came to Karaganda after many years of imprisonment. He was set free at the age of 70, following a six-year prison term. The following year he ordained Gerhard Harder, one of the spiritual leaders of the Mennonite Brethren, for the preaching ministry—soon followed by three more ordinations—Franz Ediger, Abram Friesen and David Klassen. The four men formed the leadership of the church, and David Klassen was chosen as elder by the congregation.

A time of revival followed, as it did elsewhere. In 1957, 251 people were baptised and joined the church, while Germans began to move to Karaganda from all directions. In 1958, over 100 were baptised, and within two years the congregation numbered over 900. The authorities kept constant pressure on the church and the leaders decided to try to obtain registration from the state in order to work legally. Their first and several subsequent attempts failed.

One of the severe problems for the church was lack of

space for meetings. Private houses were too small for such large numbers of people. The church managed to purchase two earth huts in different parts of the city and to remodel the interiors to create meeting houses.

Such was the spiritual hunger of the believers that they would arrive at the church early on Sunday morning in a steady stream which persisted throughout the day. The buses and trams were filled with German-speaking passengers. Often the local authorities stopped public transport to prevent people getting to services. Undeterred, they would then walk ten or more kilometers. Heinrich Woelk commented:

This Sunday stream of people soon became noticeable in the city, and when a new person in town asked where the believers were meeting almost any citizen could show him the way.[6]

Services usually lasted two hours and it could take people as long again to get home afterwards. Despite this, most would return for the evening service. There were never any empty seats. Believers who stayed at the church for the whole day would visit the sick between services, sing to them, give them an outline of the sermons and pray with them.

Heinrich Woelk summed up this spiritual phenonemon as follows:

Karaganda, until recently known as a prison city, became known as a city of believers and many who had been deprived of God's Word and fellowship with believers came and joined the group. During the same period the Baptist church mentioned earlier also grew rapidly. It already had a church building which could seat 1,000. There was also a Church Mennonite congregation with some 300 members, as well as a Lutheran congregation of several hundred.[7]

Renewed Persecution

The year 1958 brought new renewed pressure and harassment from the authorities. Government representatives attended meetings: taking down the names, addresses and work places of members of the congregation, issuing threats, and interrupting the preachers. The meeting houses were closed down and worship forbidden, but believers continued to gather for worship in each others' homes. Often the place of meeting was made known only a few hours before the time of the service. Worship always began with a prayer which included the request, 'Lord, save us from interruptions today.' If the service could be completed in peace then prayers were offered at the close: 'Lord, we thank you that we were able to hear your Word without interruption.' Thus the work of preaching, teaching, baptising and evangelism continued, despite the constant fear of punishment and reprisals.

By 1962 membership of the church exceeded 1,000, but it was in August of that year that the church suffered a major setback, exactly as was happening under the Khrushchev persecution all over the Soviet Union. Elder David Klassen was arrested, together with the two leaders of a small group of believers who belonged to the Karaganda Church, but who met in the neighbouring town of Sarani, 25 kilometers away. The authorities had to find a pretext for these arrests and hit on the idea of examining the financial dealings of the church. All the income of the church, which consisted entirely of voluntary donations, had been carefully recorded by the church leadership and they were able to prove that none of the funds had been misused. Despite this, David Klassen was accused of spending a sum of 50,000 roubles unlawfully. The authorities began to deduct payments from his pension (he was 63 years old) but as he only received 50 roubles a month it was obvious that this method of exacting punishment would last into the next century, so he was

arrested. After a long period of investigation the three men
were tried simultaneously. Many members of the Mennonite Brethren Church attended the trial.

In a lengthy speech, the prosecutor accused them of
hindering the building of Communism by spreading confu-
sion among ordinary people, preventing children from
joining atheist organisations (the Pioneers) and so on.

The first man to be accused was told that his punishment
would be less severe if he admitted his guilt and promised
not to preach any more. The poor man who had a large family to support and suffered from ill health 'confessed' his
guilt to the court and was subsequently freed on probation.
An eye-witness who was present throughout described
what happened to the second of the accused:

Then came Heinrich Wiebe. At first he was courageous, but then
he began to give in. From all sides one could hear a gentle whis-
pering: 'Brothers, sisters, let us pray!' The court was adjourned
for a short break and our brothers were led out of the courtroom
under armed guard. They passed very close to us. Suddenly there
was the sound of a cock crowing. A young man, Friedrich Hertle,
had put his hands over his mouth and crowed like a cock. He
wanted to remind the accused of Peter's betrayal. We saw how
Heinrich Wiebe flinched. But the guards did not notice anything.
After the break Wiebe was further questioned, but now he remained firm and confessed his Lord.[8]

Wiebe was sentenced to one year of imprisonment.
David Klassen spoke out decisively in defence of the faith
and remained firm throughout the trial. Because of his
previous record of imprisonment he was given a more severe sentence of three years' hard labour.

Further persecution followed. The same eye-witness
described the fate of another faithful member, Otto Wiebe,
whose family had already suffered many years of separation from their beloved husband and father.

But the storm was not yet past. Time and again, members were called to special interrogations, and before a year had passed Otto Wiebe was taken and sentenced to four years of harsh imprisonment. (He already had 12 years imprisonment behind him.) When a last opportunity was given him by the judge to defend himself, he instead stood up in his grey prison clothing, an old, quiet man, and described his conversion to all assembled, the court, the armed soldiers and his brothers and sisters in the faith.[9]

Otto Wiebe died in prison and his body was taken home for burial by his family. Hundreds of people attended his funeral in February 1964, despite a temperature of minus 30°C. His family kept all his prison letters, most of which were sermons. They form a testimony to his unshakable faith in Jesus Christ. The following is an extract from one written in September 1963.

How homeless, comfortless and empty our life would be if we did not have the glad tidings of the Gospel and peace with God! Often I am pitied for taking such a load upon myself and torturing myself in this life, not enjoying any advantages by faith in God, and for praying in vain, since I am in the same situation as all the other prisoners. Then I try to explain that, through his grace, the love of him who loved us and brought us peace impels all his children to suffer for him without complaint. I have never prayed to God for freedom, but rather for grace and strength to be faithful and meekly to do what is pleasing in his sight. I am one of the lucky ones, because in him I am rich.[10]

Many members of the Mennonite Brethren Church saw the arrest of their elder, David Klassen, as a time of testing of their own faith. The church divided into even smaller groups and the meetings were continued in about ten different locations, despite the scrutiny of the authorities. The believers became even more closely united as a fellowship. Some were afraid of the consequences of meeting illegally and started to attend the meetings at the registered Baptist Church and later became members there.

The Baptist All-Union Council (AUCECB) held a congress in Moscow in 1963 which several Mennonites attended.

There was direct pressure by the Soviet authorities to persuade Mennonite congregations to join the Baptists. Partly as a result of this, perhaps half of the 40,000 Mennonites are in the Baptist Union. In addition, others have joined the unregistered Baptists, some of whose leaders are of Mennonite origin, including some in prison.

In Karaganda the Mennonite Brethren did apply in 1964 to register their church under the umbrella of the AUCECB, while still retaining their own identity. However, this proposal was rejected by the Council on Religious Affairs, which would not agree to having more than one prayer house in the city.

The presbyter of the Baptist Church in Karaganda was instructed by the AUCECB leadership in Moscow to allow the Mennonite Brethren congregation to use the Baptist church for its services. Consequently, on Sunday afternoons German-language services were held, at which Mennonite and Baptist preachers alternated. They were attended by a large proportion of the Mennonite Brethren Church and German members of the Baptist Church. However, the Baptist leaders continued to exert pressure on the Mennonites, urging them to give up their independence and this led to many difficulties. Eventually the Mennonite Brethren Church took the decision to resume meeting in private homes, just as they had done in 1956, thereby freeing themselves from any possibility of losing their identity as an independent church. Some members still attended the Baptist services, but their status, more or less as guests, was quite different. They left a good legacy for the Baptists, in that the Sunday afternoon German-language services they had initiated continued from that time.

Better Times
In 1965 David Klassen was released from labour camp, several months early (presumably a concession in the wake of Khrushchev's dismissal) and returned to join his congre-

gation. There was great rejoicing and in an atmosphere of renewed hope for a better relationship with the authorities, the believers set about electing leadership, establishing regulations and generally consolidating the existing work. David Klassen declined to resume the leadership, so it became the responsibility of a temporary council of four ministers. At the beginning of 1966 several small congregations from outlying areas around Karaganda successfully applied to join with them. Membership continued to increase and the believers, faced once again with the familiar problem of the lack of an adequate regular meeting place, began to make this a matter of urgent prayer for the whole church.

Prayers were answered. The CRA made a major concession: in 1967 they granted registration to the Mennonite Brethren Church in Karaganda independently of the AUCECB. For the first time the Mennonite Brethren had acquired official status in the Soviet Union. In accordance with the demands of the government and as we saw in Chapter 2, the congregation had to elect a church council of three to represent it in its dealings with the state. In an election Heinrich Woelk was unanimously chosen as elder of the church; Wilhelm Matthies became chairman of the council and co-elder of the church; Jakob Siebert and David Klassen became members of the church council and assistants to the elders.

It finally became possible for the congregation to do something about a church building. The local authorities would not tolerate a church in a central location and tried to insist that it should be on the outskirts of the city. After many setbacks and much prayer and persistence on the part of the congregation, permission to renovate and convert a two-family residence was forthcoming. The church received permission in September 1968 for the work to begin. Heinrich Woelk described the building project:

On 5 September 1968 the men of the congregation were called to a meeting at which the main tasks were divided. The work began the next day. The building was almost completely demolished. But although there were no supplies of building materials or money on hand, the Lord made his presence felt and everything necessary was found in time: money, bricks, wood, cement and labourers. Not a rouble had to be borrowed.[11]

The cornerstone of the building was laid on 7th September in the context of a service of thanksgiving and prayer. The following weeks were filled with frantic activity:

There were two months before the onset of winter. Most members had already taken their holidays, but there was never a lack of workers. The pensioners and shift workers came during the day and young workers in the evening. They laboured until 10pm every day and the building was completed by the middle of November. The church services could have begun, but a new demand from the authorities delayed the proceedings. In order to satisfy the safety requirements of the fire department a tank of at least 100 cubic meters of water was needed. It was impossible to find an excavator because no construction company wanted to be involved with a church project. The next day everyone appeared with spades and shovels and set to work. In three days the excavation (3m deep, over 130 cu m altogether) was complete. A few days later the water reservoir was ready.[12]

Eighty days after the first stone had been laid there was a service of thanksgiving in the finished building, which had seating capacity for 500 and measured 200 sq m. Once again the Mennonite Brethren community had borne witness both to their neighbours and to the local authorities. Many who had mocked and criticised the building project initially had been amazed to observe the harmonious spirit of the team and to hear them singing while they worked.

The building was dedicated on 15th December 1968, and the life of the church flourished. Over the next eight years several youth groups, as many as ten Sunday school groups for children, a church choir of over 100 singers, two youth choirs and various music groups were formed. Every year between 30 and 50 baptismal candidates were accepted into the church. Forty men participated in preaching, and of these ten were ordained ministers and seven deacons.

Registration made the congregation legal, but this did not signify freedom from persecution. Throughout this period of growth the leadership of the church was subjected to pressure from the authorities. In 1976 Heinrich Woelk left the Karaganda Church and went to live in Razdelnaya in Ukraine, where he subsequently became the elder of the first Mennonite Brethren Church in that republic. He was succeeded in Karaganda by Heinrich Goerzen, who served as elder until 1985. The present leader of the Karaganda church, elected in 1986, is Alexander Becker.

Mennonites in the Soviet Union, like other Soviet evangelicals and indeed many Mennonite communities in the USA, are characterised by their deep piety. Generally their entire social life revolves around the church. Attendance at worship is expected several times a week. Entertainment, such as attending concerts, cinemas or theatres, is regarded as sinful. Marriage between believers and non-believers is not permitted. If such marriages take place despite warnings, the offender is excommunicated. Church members are required to submit to the decisions of the church and not to discuss internal church matters with non-members. They are expected to abstain from smoking and alcohol and to be modest in their form of dress and conduct. Great emphasis is placed on maintaining Christian witness within the family through family prayers, especially at meal times, and Bible study.

All basic questions concerning the life of the church, such as elections, acceptance of members, excommunication and church discipline, changes or additions to the rules, are decided by the whole church. Day-to-day matters in the life of the church are decided by the elder with the advice, where necessary, of the church council.

Ministers are chosen by the church and consecrated by

ordained ministers. Deacons are elected and ordained to carry out practical service in the church, such as maintaining the church building and looking after the sick. They assist the ministers in communion services, serve communion to the sick in their homes and assist with baptisms. They can be called upon to preach if necessary. They also concern themselves with the material welfare of needy church members. Since all 'charitable' work by the churches is banned, the deacons have to carry out these tasks with the utmost discretion. Ministers, deacons and the elder all serve the church without pay.

One of the characteristic features of the life of the church is its emphasis on communal prayer. Prayer meetings are held on Saturdays. After a short talk, several of the men lead in prayer, taking a theme from the Bible. Prayers are offered individually, but believers are encouraged to keep their prayers short and to the point. Each year begins with a week of structured prayer. Bible studies are held on week nights and play an especially important role in teaching young people.

Sunday worship generally lasts for at least two hours, during which there are three or four sermons. If there is a shortage of ministers, they read classic sermons by someone such as Spurgeon, if texts are available. The choir sings, and there is Communion once a month on the first Sunday.

According to Soviet law, the only activity permitted to a local congregation is worship within the four walls of a registered building. All other activities such as youth work, Sunday schools, courses for ministers, publishing, religious education courses and evangelism are forbidden. Despite this, all these activities go on in the Karaganda church, putting the whole church, and in particular the organisers of such activities, at great risk. The religious education of young children is primarily the responsibility of parents, but in addition Sunday schools are organised mainly by young women. Groups of about 20 children are formed according to their age and location. The main content of Sunday school is a Bible story, singing and the learning of Bible verses and Psalms. In the Karaganda church between 1974 and 1976 more than ten groups were formed, each led by one or two women. Young men often help with singing and instrumental music. The Sunday school teachers share their experiences and help each other. Many of the young people who ask for baptism testify that the seeds of faith which led to their conversion were sown in Sunday school classes.

Young people of 16 and over meet weekly and a mature younger Christian leads them. Many young people who are not members of the church attend and the goal of the youth work is to bring them to a knowledge of their own sinfulness, the need for repentance and salvation through Christ and to nurture them in the faith. This is achieved mainly through Bible study, using available evangelical books. There is a great emphasis on memorising Bible verses, songs and poems. Their parents and grandparents learned that this was a unique and vital way of preserving the faith in times of adversity and they are anxious to instil this lesson in their children. The youth meetings also have talks on practical Christianity and ethics. Older members are invited from time to time to talk about their experiences of the faith and all support the work by prayer.

Singing has always played an important part in the Mennonite communities. During especially difficult years when families were divided, fathers were absent and there was no preaching, mothers sang hymns to their children as a means of communicating the faith. When church services were resumed in the 1950s, ministers tried every means to find hymn books, supplemented by a domestic copying industry producing hundreds of books. The lack of hymn books meant that believers have learned much by heart, a disadvantage leading to a new strength. In the same way, they laboriously copied out portions of the Bible and distributed them. The singing of the choir is a treasured feature and

choir members, even more than others, are expected to
lead exemplary lives. Singing is sometimes accompanied by
various instruments, but these are not allowed to dominate
the singing. Both choir and church orchestras must practise
every week.

Mennonites have no Bible or training school for church
workers in the Soviet Union. Since the mid-1950s when the
rebuilding of the church began, older and more experienced church workers have sought to help the younger and
less experienced. Some of the older men who attended
training courses in their youth have been able to pass on
their knowledge to young ministers. Heinrich Woelk had
such training and describes in his book a series of meetings
which took place in 1973, when he and Walter Matthies
taught the essentials of homiletics to a group of ten young
men between the ages of 18 and 30. When the authorities
made it impossible to continue such gatherings, the young
men worked on by themselves.

Someone found a cache of theological books which
provided basic guidelines, resulting in a plan of study: introduction to the Bible; church history; homiletics;
apologetics, dogmatics and exegesis. Because there was
only one copy of each book the material was summarised.
The subjects were divided among the participants and each
prepared a subject and taught the others. The meetings
were held in different locations to avoid the unwelcome attention of the authorities. Older ministers gave advice on
specific issues. Soon the young men were sent out into outlying villages to give trial sermons for discussion and
appraisal. After a year another seven joined the first ten. In
1976 a second group of ten received instruction from members of the first group. Most are now ministers in Mennonite Brethren congregations.

In January 1981 H. Neufeld, an old teacher from the
church in Karaganda, wrote the following:

Among our young people we have a wonderful supply of church

workers. Our old leaders will soon have to make room for them. We must decrease; they must increase.[13]

In the mid-1970s some leaders boldly decided to found a regular journal for young people. The first issue of an unofficial monthly journal entitled *Der Jugend Freund* (Friend of Youth) appeared in January 1974. In the first year one issue only appeared. It was read aloud in the youth meetings of the Karaganda Church. Its contents included an introduction to the history of the Mennonite Church, a variety of themes for discussion among young people, poems, songs and commentary on difficult Bible passages. It quickly became very popular and the next year five issues appeared. Now many congregations in different places receive it. In 1977 a second monthly publication, *Gemeinde* (The Congregation), was begun, intended for the whole church community. For the first two years it was edited and produced at Razdelnaya, Ukraine, but it subsequently moved. There are now ten numbers a year and it reaches most churches. There is a section entitled 'From our churches', which ensures that congregations are in touch with one another.

The Mennonite Brethren take the view that all governmental authority, even that of atheists, is ordained by God and that the church should not therefore oppose the authorities. This does not mean, as we have seen, that they are prepared to compromise in what they regard as their basic Christian duty, as for example, in teaching Christianity to children. However, it is the manner in which they set about these duties which distinguishes them to some extent from other branches of the evangelical faith. Heinrich Woelk illustrates this as follows:

Mennonite parents concern themselves with the spiritual upbringing of their children who gather in small Sunday school groups to remain unobtrusive. In the service the children sit with their parents and again the children do not stand out. When the question of joining the Young Pioneers arises, the father or mother goes to the school principal or teacher and asks that the child be excused from this activity, because it would be against their conscience. Let the children choose their own path later, but now they are the parents' responsibility.[14]

In recent years, contacts have been re-established with fellow believers outside the Soviet Union. The Mennonite Central Committee (Akron, Pennsylvania) has taken the lead in supplying moral, spiritual and, when possible, material help to the scattered churches in the Soviet Union, not excluding such remote areas as Kazakhstan. Contacts with the Mennonite World Conference are now opening up as well.

Some Mennonites, for whom Russia and the Soviet Union have been home for two centuries, have 're-emigrated' to West Germany under an agreement between the Soviet and German governments, so they have been able to return to their ancestral homelands or areas not so far away from them. With the general increase in restrictions after 1979, this emigration movement was much reduced, as it was also for Soviet Jews at the same time, but not before Mennonite and German piety was re-injected into the Federal Republic. The overflowing of spiritual revival among fundamentalist communities in the USSR can produce a harvest in more than one land.

Perhaps Soviet Mennonites, with their quiet nature and their ability to work prodigiously at caring husbandry on often intractable soil, carry a certain protection, even locally a status as models of productivity. This leads, in turn, to some concessions on military service. If they are allowed their churches, they will not raise their heads as 'dissidents', so are not among the most persecuted of religious minorities at this moment. The threat is always there in the background, especially when the authorities, as they do periodically, review the success of the religious communities with young people—and no minority has had more success in keeping its youth within the fellowship.

Even under Soviet conditions, they have proved that it is possible to build a Christian community within an alien environment and to maintain it. Mennonite leaders are, however, aware that they must gradually introduce Russian into the structure of their thought in order to guarantee the long-term future of their faith. No Mennonite, looking back over the troubles of the last decades, will want to disturb the present equilibrium, and they will all continue to pray that the Soviet authorities will not do so.

Chapter 5

Moscow Baptists: A World Centre

Whether it is God's sense of humour or his assurance to mankind, we cannot tell—probably the latter—but the distinction is of little importance. In a land where there were no Protestants until just over 100 years ago, in a vast urban agglomeration which is now the heartland of atheism and where the first proper evangelical church did not open its doors until well into this century—there now exists one of the world's liveliest and most flourishing churches. While Ukraine contains far more Baptists than does the Russian Republic, the country's largest church is now in central Moscow. The lack of other Baptist churches within the city limits serves to concentrate the life of the community.

Despite the onslaught of Stalin against religion, by the time of his death in 1953 the Moscow Baptist Church had grown from a handful in 1909 to some 4,500 baptised members, not to mention thousands, probably tens of thousands, more who came under its influence. The growth to about 5,200 members in the 1980s may seem modest, but it is in reality a significant one, for the statistics conceal a hidden growth. In the intervening years some 17 new churches have successfully sought registration in the Moscow region. Therefore fewer people need to trek all the way to Moscow for services, as they can now have their own.

The true growth, for which there are no figures, far exceeds the bald statistic of the official membership.

The church at No 3 Maly Vuzovsky Pereulok has been central for Moscow for 70 years, but since World War II it has been central for the whole Soviet Union and now, increasingly and in a very real sense, for the world. There can be few churches, discounting purely tourist traffic in the historical cathedrals of Europe, which receive such a constant stream of foreign guests, the vast majority of whom come with the genuine intention of worshipping and attempting to have some form of fellowship with local believers. The offices in the same building which house the organisation called the All-Union Council of Evangelical Christians and Baptists (AUCECB) are a hive of activity at all times when they are open and when services are not taking place. Baptists pour in from all corners of the Soviet Union, many on official business, but some also coming on the offchance of meeting foreigners, with whom they can have conversations, or simply in the hope of begging some Christian literature, if there is no common language to be found. Every foreign visitor who comes out of service hours must be individually and politely received, which puts an immense strain on the personnel of the 'foreign department'.

A Look at the Building

Physically the Moscow Baptist Church is inadequate for its purpose. The equivalent First Baptist Church in an American city would have a capacity three times the size, perhaps with a skyscraper office block attached. It is said that at maximum capacity (most of the services) over 2,000 people can squeeze into it, but less than half of these are seated. The impression is of permanent discomfort, though this is not immediately evident because the people make so light of it.

We shall later describe what happens when it is full, but let us spend a moment looking at it empty. Similar non-conformist churches exist in many English provincial towns. A balcony with seats runs round two sides and the back, from which you can look down on the rows of wooden benches facing the Lord's Table. Those who arrive early enough can sit down, unlike in an Orthodox church. There is no cross on the table, which is on floor level, but there are two candlesticks. From either side of it two low flights of wooden stairs run up to about half the height of the gallery. This elevates the several pastors who are going to take an active part in leading the service high above the body of the congregation. When their turn comes to pray or preach they walk to the pulpit, which forms the front part of the platform and is decorated with the fleshy leaves of some potted plant directly above the table. This platform recedes into an apse with three stained glass windows, two of which have pale geometrical patterns, flanking the central one which proclaims the Russian words *Bog yest lyubov* ('God is love') emblazoned on it. Opposite this, at the back of the church, 'The Lord be with you all' stands out in large sign-painted letters, above the main door directly beneath the central part of the gallery. This latter encloses a rostrum where the 'regent' (choirmaster) stands in front of his choir. Behind them are ranged the organ pipes, a familiar feature to every Western visitor, but of course quite alien to the tradition of the Russian Orthodox Church. Take away the Russian inscriptions and possibly the potted plant and you would not know you were in the Soviet Union at all.

Yet this appearance is deceptive. Soviet Protestants cannot be considered a foreign graft which has never developed its own root stock. For several decades, both before and after the Revolution, the Russian Baptists have brought an essential and expanding aspect of Christianity to the land; when the church is full of people, you could be nowhere else but in the Soviet Union.

A History of Growth

The word 'Baptist' applied to this Moscow church, deviates from the strictest accuracy. The correct title, virtually never used except on official documents, is the 'Moscow Evangelical Christian and Baptist Congregation'—a cumbersome name that indicates the mixed origin of the movement. Russian Protestantism began more or less simultaneously under different influences in three widely-separated areas of the Tsarist Empire. The beginnings, according to the Baptists' own official history, were in the 1860s. Lutheran and Reformed pastors were working, along with Mennonites, especially among immigrants in Ukraine at this time. A Scotsman named Melville conducted an active ministry for the British and Foreign Bible Society in the Caucasus. Very influentially (for later history) Lord Radstock, an English leader of the Plymouth Brethren, led a mission among the aristocracy of the then-capital city, St Petersburg, a decade later.

The St Petersburg group called themselves 'Evangelical Christians', while the Ukrainians became 'Baptists'. There was never any serious doctrinal divergence between them, but a difference of 'style' kept them apart. From 1944, however, they have been united, partly as a result of a helping hand from the Soviet authorities. Here we adopt the common usage of referring to the whole united movement as 'Baptists'. One of its official historians (anonymous, but using the initials 'RK') writes movingly of this unity in his history of the Moscow church, published in *Bratsky Vestnik* ('Fraternal Messenger'), the official bi-monthly organ of the Russian Baptists, in 1982–83.[1] He describes it as a great river, flowing with power and purpose. When you examine its origins, he says several tributaries have flowed into it, each of which may at some earlier time have been obscured by overhanging bushes or broken by stony rapids; but behind each of them lies a secret spring of pure water.

This history emphasises both the late beginning and humble origins of the Moscow community, as compared with that in Leningrad. After visiting Moscow, Lord Radstock complained that the aristocracy there was deaf to his message; when the movement did begin with some modest Bible Society work in the 1880s the influence was exclusively among the working class.

The early days were very uncertain. The first meeting place was a hotel room, but under the watchful and hostile eyes of the authorities there was no permanence. Various Evangelical Christian and Baptist groups met separately during the 'Pobedonostsev period' (1880–1905), called after the feared 'Over-Procurator' of the Holy Synod of the Orthodox Church, the last man to try to force religious conformism upon the Russian people and at the same time to break the would-be unity of the Baptists and Evangelical Christians. Initiating a precedent later to be followed in more brutal form by Stalin (which the official historian cannot mention), exile to Siberia for many of the activists was the equivalent of the state's paying their missionary expenses. There was less control in the vast expanses of the countryside, so exiles from Moscow were soon planting seeds in the outposts of empire.

From 1905 conditions eased considerably in Moscow. Evangelical Christians and Baptists between them established more than one regular prayer house and some Christian publishing even began. The next 12 years were a period of significant growth, though World War I was a difficult time, as the regime tended to look upon the Baptists as people who shared the 'German faith' of the enemy.

The deposition of the Tsar in March 1917 and the withdrawal from the war presented the Baptists with an unparalleled opportunity, however. In the very next month the Evangelical Christians acquired the premises at Maly Vuzovsky Pereulok, which were eventually to become the national headquarters for the united movement. For six months the whole country enjoyed both true religious liberty and a nascent democracy which was unique both in previous and subsequent history.

Nevertheless, the years immediately after the advent of Soviet power with the Revolution of October 1917 did not witness the disaster for the Baptists which the Orthodox Church experienced. In 1922 the Baptist Union was able to organise ten commissions to develop various aspects of its growth: evangelism, publishing, music, material aid, pastoral care of preachers, preparation of other church workers and evangelists, moral education, finance, judicial affairs and church order.[2] One of the Bible schools was in Moscow. No doubt the official historian cannot mention this multifarious activity because of the contrast it presents with the stark restrictions of today. There were at the time bitter divisions within the Baptist community over the obligation to do military service.

The advent of Stalinism saw a rapid decline of all these activities. Indeed, by the outbreak of World War II, the very existence of the Baptist Church, along with all other religious denominations, was under threat. It is possible that even the Moscow premises at Maly Vuzovsky closed during this time (the official history says virtually nothing about activities there during the 1930s). Mikhail Orlov conducted services there during the war. Following the withdrawal of the threat of the German occupation of Moscow, not only did worship resume more than its former vigour—now bolstered by patriotic fervour and the almost universal return to religion during those years—but also the Soviet authorities actively encouraged the formal union of the Evangelical Christians and Baptists at their single centre in 1944. The presence of a mere 45 delegates at a congress to establish this unity indicates just how difficult circumstances were at that time. There was a move the next year which formally brought the Pentecostals into this union, but it never achieved the smoothness or permanent success of the union between the Evangelical Christians and the Baptists. About half the Mennonites also joined this union in 1963 (see p.90).

Nevertheless, the end of the war saw a united Evangelical church in Moscow, the size of which was without precedent on Russian soil. It developed with great zeal and
spirituality, though not without its rough times, caused not
only by theological differences with the Pentecostals, who
were truly the junior partner in the union, but also by major
extraneous factors.

The years of Nikita Khrushchev's ascendancy (1959–64)
saw a major organised campaign against religion. Perhaps
the Baptists suffered worse from this than any other single
denomination, though the deprivations of the Orthodox
cannot have been far behind. The Soviet regime forced new
internal regulations upon the Baptist community which
were a direct negation of basic evangelical traditions—no
evangelism in sermons, a minimum of baptisms under the
age of 30, for example. These split the Baptists nationwide,[3] and the schism persists right up to the present. In
many areas whole congregations separated from the union
and in the next chapter we detail a specific instance.
Moscow could not fail to be riven in the 1960s by what was
happening elsewhere. But it was also the church where the
official leadership was in place and we must take note of the
fact that it received official backing from the authorities,
despite the clause in the Soviet Constitution which proclaims the separation of church and state.

Even the official history of the Moscow Baptist Church
notes that 11 members left it to join the 'Reform Baptists'
(see p 119). We can only guess at the internal tensions
which led to this move, though we have much more detail of
the major upheavals of the time in various provincial
centres. At Dedovsk, in the Moscow Region, for example,
a vigorous unregistered community had long since existed.
In the 1950s Pastor Rumachik, its leader, repeatedly but
unsuccessfully applied for registration. Persecution followed and to this day they have no building, despite eventual registration outside the Baptist Union.

Nevertheless, the outward appearance of the Moscow Baptist community to the stream of visitors during the 1960s and 70s was one of stability. The Baptist World Alliance was only one group among many others who implied that the disagreements were over relatively trivial issues of personalities and control of the Baptist movement. Detailed discussion in the BWA of the essential issues seems never to have taken place, even to this day.

One of the founders of the union, Yakov Zhidkov, continued as 'honorary' pastor of the Moscow Baptist Church until his death in old age, in 1966. His son, Mikhail, became 'second pastor' of the Moscow Baptist Church in 1964, a position for which he was theologically qualified many times over. However his two separate spells abroad, one in England (Spurgeons College) and the other in Canada (McMaster University) implied political reliability as well as theological competence. In 1966 Mikhail Zhidkov became the senior pastor of the Moscow church. The positions in the hierarchy of the AUCECB, which we are not here considering, were quite different. In this Pastor Zhidkov became a vice-president and frequently travelled abroad.

Just in case there is any lingering doubt about the reality of the growth of this remarkable Christian community, it is worth quoting one of the unending cohorts of Soviet propagandists who are determined to show that religion is dying out in their country. Lev Mitrokhin, an atheist writer who visited London in September 1968, writes unambiguously of the growth of the Baptist community during the Soviet period.[4] It occurred 'notably' during the 1920s and 'continued' during the 1930s and 'rapidly' developed during the post-war years. His later claim that it 'ceased' during the 1960s and 1970s is manifestly in line with the cessation of registration following the Khrushchev purges, rather than the actual numbers involved.

The Spiritual Life of a Great Church

'The Moscow Baptist Church is nothing other than a show church.' One hears the accusation with boring frequency. Yes, it is true that it is convenient for the Soviet authorities to have a church close to the centre of Moscow in which the myriad of foreign Protestant visitors can feel at home. Yes, it is true that its pastors have never, in over 40 post-war years, put a word out of line which would imply criticism of Soviet domestic or foreign policy. Yes, one can sometimes hear Soviet peace progaganda from the pulpit. Yes, this was the first registered church to hold youth services which, even now, are strictly speaking illegal. No, it is not true that there is no vital spiritual life beneath the surface of this unique phenomenon. Indeed, thousands of Soviet citizens and some foreigners have been brought to a commitment to Christ by what they have heard and experienced within these walls. There have also been demonstrable tensions in recent years. Baptists from other areas of the Soviet Union, where persecution is much worse, have come to unfurl their banners listing the names of imprisoned loved ones before the eyes of foreign guests, and have been expelled from the building. Billy Graham witnessed such a scene in 1982, as did a delegation from the National Council of Churches (USA) in 1984. Let us not discount the importance of a place where Soviet Baptists from the provinces are virtually certain of meeting foreign believers, perhaps for the first time in the lives of either of them.

There were in the 1950s six services a week, three on Sundays, three on week days, all full to bursting point. In the 1960s this number was reduced to five, supposedly to relieve the pressure on the pastors who would now have to produce fewer sermons each week (18 down to 15 as there are three in each service). Now the number is restored to six. The uninhibited outpouring of prayer and singing, guided by three impassioned Bible-based sermons, spread over a two-hour span and uniting a vast congregation of people, is an unparalelled spiritual experience for those who participate.

An official Russian Baptist publication put this quaintly but succinctly in English:

Sermon is the main divine service of the New Testament Church. The good message of the salvation through Jesus Christ refreshes the joy of salvation in our hearts and leads to this joy all those who have not experienced it yet.[5]

None of the three sermons in a two-hour service must be over-long, because each 40-minute segment must leave ample time for singing and prayer. The conviction with which these sermons are delivered more than compensates for the lack of theological sophistication which is inevitable when one considers that there has been no residential seminary for Russian Baptists for 60 years and that the vast store of theological works available to pastors elsewhere simply for the asking at a public library is unknown to their Soviet counterparts. In fact, listening to these sermons, one often asks oneself the question whether conventional theological learning helps in any practical way to communicate the Gospel. Perhaps living out the Gospel in a hostile environment enables the preacher to do it with that much more conviction.

Singing seems to take, if that were possible, even more of the weight during divine service. Since the 1960s the technical standard of their choral singing has improved considerably.[6] As Walter Sawatsky wrote:

Soviet evangelicals cannot imagine a religious gathering without music and singing. The birth of a baby, a wedding, even a funeral are accompanied by singing. Conferences and congresses are unimaginable without singing. For me, the reverberations of more than 1,000 male voices lifted in praise remain one of the unforgettable experiences of the 1974 AUCECB congress.[7]

In the 1950s there was one choir. 1963–64 saw the establishment of a second, to relieve the immense strain of rehearsing for and singing five or six services a week.

Despite the existence of regulations limiting the use of instruments in church other than the organ, which indeed were put rigorously into effect in many other places, the Moscow Baptist Church established an orchestra of folk-instruments to accompany the second choir. Perhaps this could happen only in a church frequented by foreign visitors, but it is good that the pastors exploited the slightly more liberal atmosphere which resulted from the church's being in the public eye. Now there is a third choir which concentrates more on classical music. It sings both *a capella* and with the accompaniment of a chamber orchestra. There is yet a fourth group, the Moscow Youth Choir, which produced a gramophone record for export, the sleeve of which describes it as relatively new, with about 75 voices in their late teens and early twenties. The accompanying photographs bear witness to an activity which would certainly be considered illegal in many other places.

Many visitors have described the prayer of a rare intensity, led from the pulpit, accompanied by deep emotion and heightened by the fluttering of slips of paper containing prayer requests from the gallery to people below, who in their turn forward them to the front. In such a public place, before the eyes and ears of the atheist authorities, there is inevitably a limitation on the subject matter of prayers (none for prisoners, for example, though these do occur in private); yet what is unspoken is not unheard in the mind and this prayer embraces society and the world. The congregation presents flowers to the constant stream of newly baptised. This growing community maintains its unity especially through three services of Holy Communion a month, and the pastors take the sacrament to those who are housebound.

Here is a personal description of Christmas with the Moscow Baptists:

The service was filled with the keen sense of quiet anticipation which one finds in Christmas Eve in England. The congregation's singing of 'Silent Night' remains most vividly in my memory of that evening. It was taken so slowly that one had, almost, to breathe in the middle of words, but it was remarkable how this most Teutonic of melodies had taken on a new Slavonic lease of life. It brought home to me more sharply than anything had done before how completely the Baptist faith has married Slavonic temperament to the ethos of Protestantism.[8]

Inner Tensions

Despite the comparative liberalism of the Soviet authorities towards the Moscow Baptist Church, there have been tensions over the years, as we saw above. After the Reform Baptist schism of the 1960s there were sometimes other tensions of a fundamental nature which broke the apparently untroubled surface of Moscow Baptist life. In 1978 the Soviet authorities investigated the 'criminal activity' of one of the church's youth leaders, Alexander Semchenko, then aged 30, and two of his fellow-activists. They had allegedly set up a secret studio where they recorded foreign Christian radio broadcasts and music for copying on to cassette and distributing to those who requested such encouragement.

No court proceedings followed the original investigation, but on 24th January 1984 Semchenko received a three-year sentence for distributing Christian literature. By the time of this second case the church leadership had already expelled him from the congregation, just as the Leningrad leaders had recently expelled Valeri Barinov for even more notable activities.[9] Church leaders and the state acted in sorry concert, with a lengthy and slanderous article appearing in a Soviet daily newspaper, Trud ('Labour').[10] Lyuba, Semchenko's wife, has asked Christians in the West to take up her husband's case, but his name has remained virtually unknown.

Disproving the contention often made by church leaders

who visit the Soviet Union that only members of unregistered congregations fall foul of Soviet law, other members of the Moscow church have also been in trouble in recent years. Alexander Komar was arrested in 1981 for distributing Christian literature and in 1985 Vasili Pali completed a three-year sentence on a similar charge.

Model Workers

The continuing low educational level of Soviet Baptists is attributable not merely to the appeal of the movement to workers, as may appear on the surface, though this is certainly part of the truth. There is also systematic prohibition of higher education for Christian teenagers; they are inevitably assigned to menial jobs. For many years the Baptist Church was unable even minimally to compensate by providing theological education for its own leaders, a privilege which had been extended to the Russian Orthodox Church immediately after World War II.

A handful of Baptist pastors did secure permission to study abroad from the late 1950s onwards, but this was a concession only sporadically granted. In recent years the leadership has urgently sought permission to establish a permanent residential seminary, but so far in vain, though they have reportedly been told to look for a suitable site. If this happened, it would probably be in Moscow and would further enrich the life of the Baptist community there. Soviet law forbids 'itinerant ministers' from preaching to congregations other than their own, but there would be a way round this if the students were resident in the capital city. As it is, the leadership did obtain permission to establish a correspondence course in the 1970s, and the students do come together for very short periods, mainly for examinations, twice a year. The 25 who graduated in 1985 brought the total number to over 300.

It is not as easy as it used to be for Soviet atheist propagandists to dismiss the Baptists as coming from the worst-educated strata of society. At those times when atheist writers have enjoyed some greater latitude to write the truth, such as during the late 1960s, something of the true contribution of Baptists to Soviet society has emerged. If this is applicable to scattered communities in distant parts of the Soviet Union, it is likely to be even more so of Moscow, where believers are so easily able to benefit from such a warm sense of community in which there is much mutual encouragement. Lev Mitrokhin wrote in 1966: 'As a rule, Baptists work conscientiously and strictly observe labour discipline.'[11] Another atheist author, E.G. Filimonov, devotes no fewer than 15 pages to a section entitled 'Work as a religious duty', in which he quotes a Baptist saying that work is a 'loom on which a man's soul is woven'.[12]

The Baptists' high standards of personal morality are widely recognised both inside and outside the community. Drinking, smoking and sexual immorality are strongly discouraged, a policy which makes all the more ludicrous the accusations of wild excesses which garnish Soviet atheist attacks when the pressure is on. An atheist author once quoted, without disapproval, a Soviet medical worker as saying:

I have had to cure people of alcoholism and traumas received as a result of drinking bouts. I am convinced that the only way of stopping drunkenness is the spread of the Baptist faith. A teetotal Baptist is far more use to society than a drunken atheist.[13]

If only Mr Gorbachov had the imagination to do so, he could harness a most powerful ally in his anti-alcohol campaign, for the Russian Baptists, almost alone in Soviet society, illustrate just what it is possible to achieve with the right motivation. If he cannot bring himself to find this out from other means, perhaps he should start by reading some of the official atheist literature of 20 years ago (to which his wife contributed).

The Moscow Baptist community is high profile for the

Soviet regime, as well as for foreigners. Its vigour, high standards of personal morality and basic loyalty of its leaders to the Soviet system must surely impress themselves on the leaders of the Kremlin.

Chapter 6

Ukrainian Baptists: Cathedral of the Forest

Around the grave there were two concentric circles of people, quite distinct from each other. The family was burying the coffin in sorrow, but beneath their sobbing, prayers, gentle reading and quiet songs there was a calm note of thankfulness. Then the outer circle threatened to break through the first, ready to snatch the very corpse out of the coffin. Shouting and howling in indignation, they drowned the dignity of the relatives.

The old man had held out against the Christian love of his wife and children for years. Pride of the local atheists, he was a living example to illustrate that God did not always win in a divided family. So they thought. Illness had struck him suddenly, in the full vigour of health. It was short, but not so short that he had no time to repent on his deathbed. Love had triumphed. His former friends were powerless to do more than register their indignation and disbelief when the funeral turned out to be a Christian one.

After the event the local believers wondered if they could have done even more to witness to the atheists. It had been a triumph, nevertheless the disgraceful din at the graveside could not have been all that pleasing to God. 'We'll start a brass band!' said someone, 'They won't be able to drown that.'

And so they did. They had neither players nor instruments, let alone scores to follow, but they did not let that daunt their prayers to God. A year later the band was ready to give its first performance. The whole enterprise, involving largely young people, seemed to gain spontaneous momentum. Some came to play and stayed to pray. It brought its members to that harmony of belief which swelled to a crescendo to lead others to the faith. By 1977, ten years after the funeral, there were so many instrumentalists they had to divide into two bands. They played not only at funerals, but there were now enough to play at weddings and to lead the many occasions of worship as well. They were strong enough to lead an immense throng of 2,000 people in an open-air service. Their fame preceded them to far-away places. Nothing daunted by being beaten up by the police at Oryol and losing some of their instruments, they travelled 600 miles from their home base in Kharkov to a wedding at Mazadze in Georgia. Some local believers were afraid. What would the neighbours do? But the occasion brought, as did so many others, a shower of blessings. And it had all begun because the atheists thought they could ruin an old man's Christian funeral.

Ukraine's Evangelicals

The Soviet Republic of Ukraine has a different language and culture from Russia, and many Ukrainians would like independence, even though there is much overlap in the history of the two regions. The Ukrainians are a very religious people and the three main streams—of Orthodoxy, Catholicism and Protestantism—all have a major following. Possibly as many as half of all the Protestants in the Soviet Union live in Ukraine, with the Baptists being especially active: so much so that there are no less than three registered churches in Kharkov (Kharkiv in Ukrainian). Why it should be so much better off in this respect than Moscow itself, where there are more Baptists in total, is not known. In this, the second largest city of Ukraine (after Kiev), the 1½ million people have three Orthodox churches, but the Pentecostals are unregistered and there is no synagogue, despite the presence of a Jewish community.

I am holding a beautiful hand-produced volume celebrating 125 years of the Baptist faith in Ukraine (1852–1977) and illustrating life in Kharkov in particular. Enlivened by some stunning photographs, it tells an inspiring story of Christian growth, especially during recent years, despite the unceasing hostility of the atheist authorities. This is the most substantial of an uninterrupted stream of documents over the last 25 years that would enable us to write a whole book about that one city.

The volume, entitled *Eben-ezer* ('Hitherto hath the Lord helped us', 1 Sam 7:12) looks lovingly back on some of the heroes of the past: Ivan Onishchenko, the first to be baptised by immersion in 1852, and Ivan Ryaboshapka, whom a Tsarist official reported 96 times in one year for his illegal Christian activities. But more important is a graph showing the growth of the total of evangelical believers in Ukraine from one in 1852 to no less than a quarter of a million in 1977 and still rising rapidly, with the whole of the substantial growth being in the Soviet period (a few thousand in 1917, 100,000 by 1927).

We have written so far in this book of registered Baptists, but this jubilee volume was produced by the unregistered (illegal) Baptists. It is not just that the registered churches are too few and too small in size to accommodate all those who wish to worship, though this is true enough. There are some substantial differences between the two groups, also. There are none, it must be emphasised, over the essential dogmas of the evangelical faith, but there are major divergences of opinion over attitudes to the atheist authorities. The activities of the two groups therefore sometimes overlap. They sometimes share each other's fellowship at worship and more often in private.

How then did this split occur? It is a relatively recent

phenomenon. To put it into the most basic but provocative terms, the unregistered Baptists are actually more 'Leninist' than their registered counterparts, pursuing with devotion the principle of the Soviet Constitution from the earliest times that there should be 'separation of church and state'.[1] The registered Baptists are more flexible and believe in going along with certain state requirements in order to weather storms and establish harbours on safer shores.

Such divergent attitudes were found to exist in most religious communities from the earliest Soviet period, but with the Baptists they did not cause a division into two separate camps until the early 1960s. Nikita Khrushchev, when he came to power after Stalin, found a religious revival well under way. Anti-constitutional laws forcing religious communities to register with the state to achieve legality were simply being ignored. His native Ukraine, even more than most other areas, was being engulfed by waves of unregulated religious activity, particularly in those parts which had so recently come under German domination.

The authorities intimidated some Baptist leaders into accepting new restrictions (see p 106). The reaction was immediate and came especially strongly from Ukraine. Boris Zdorovets from Kharkov was one of the initiators of resistance to the renewed persecution and Pastors Georgi Vins and Gennadi Kryuchkov from Kiev soon joined him in what shortly became a nationwide movement, such were the organisational ability and tenacity of these men. As we saw in the previous chapter, the recognised Baptist leadership declined to go along with them, resulting in schism.

In its incessant attacks against the new movement the state dubbed its members *Initsiativniki* (initiators), a not particularly uncomplimentary name which, nevertheless, they did not much use of themselves. They called their independent movement the 'Council of Churches of the Evangelical Christians and Baptists' (CCECB), as opposed to the official All-Union Council of Evangelical Christians and Baptists (AUCECB). But in their own common parlance the *Initsiativniki* often called themselves 'young Baptists', so much were they synonymous with a youth movement. Walter Sawatsky, the acknowledged authority on the subject,[2] calls them 'Reform Baptists' and we will follow him in this.

After the fall of Khrushchev, the pressure on the official Baptist leadership became considerably less; but they had forfeited the confidence of the Reform Baptists, for whom persecution continued unabated—as it does up to this day. Relations between individuals of the two groups remained friendly, but many of the numerous young people who wanted to join the Baptist movement found the continuing restrictions in the registered churches too irksome and the very freedom of the Reform Baptists became a powerful tool of evangelism in Soviet conditions.

It would not be true to say, as the accusation has often run, that the Reform Baptists deliberately flouted Soviet authority and 'courted martyrdom'. Rather, they experienced the liberating truth of the Gospel which had made them free, in fulfilment of the assurance of St John (8:32).

There is no note of 'anti-Sovietism', only of demands for a fair deal, in their dozens of communications which we have and they have frequently gone as far as to ask for registration, provided they do not thereby have to compromise their activities by, for example, restricting youth work. Such gestures have been countered by systematic rejection leading to further persecution. Nevertheless, in this chapter we shall concentrate on the growth which has complemented the persecution, rather than on the brutal details of the ceaseless physical attacks by the authorities against the believers.

Spontaneous Conversion
Around Kharkov on many occasions the 'cathedral of the forest' witnessed gatherings of up to 2,000 people, sometimes undisturbed by the police. No registered church

could have encompassed such crowds. Of course, such open-air meetings were not possible in winter because of the cold, but that made summer all the more festive when it came. The May-Day holiday falls conveniently to mark the change in seasons and here, as in other places, believers have Christianised the 'workers' holiday' to hold a day-long exultation of preaching and song.

One young girl heard about the May youth festival (*mayevka*) and visited it while still an unbeliever. She found herself among would-be friends who had come from as far afield as the Donbas, the Crimea and even Russia. By contrast with the registered churches, young people and children could participate freely, and no one prevented them from opening their hearts to the Lord. Everyone sat in rows on the grass to share their food and the simplicity and beauty of the occasion must have been a little like when Christ fed the 5,000. She wrote:

I felt the desire, or rather the curiosity, to see young believers who felt constrained inside houses; I wanted to know what sort of people these were who feared no threats and held their services beneath the open sky. These questions drew me to this numerous fellowship of young people. There, for the first time, I discovered that God was not something distant and unobtainable, but that he was close to men, because when believers prayed fervently from their hearts, they seemed to be speaking with One who, though invisible, was right beside them, One who listened so attentively and then answered. Then I came to love these meetings very much. I admired those who believed in God so avidly, fearlessly and sincerely. At one of these forest meetings I gave my heart to Christ.[3]

This girl later on wrote a poem to the forest which found its way into the jubilee volume. It began:

> Your spring-green dress now clothes you,
> As you smile a welcome towards us;
> The embrace of your branches enfolds us

Under the sky-blue nave of heaven.
To us you are dear in this spring time,
A broad and spacious house of prayer,
With scent of oak and resinous pine,
And fragrant flowers, a choir of birds.[4]

This girl, like hundreds of others, came to Christ through a 'corridor of salvation'. We can see her, or someone like her, in a photograph, head buried in hands, in the very act of confession to God. Individual repentance, expressed with the sincerity of deep emotion, marks the moment of conversion for these children of God. Baptism signals the final entry into the fellowship, but there is a narrower gate before this—literally a corridor which the believers open up to let someone pass to the front through the tight throng with the words, 'Let him pass! Make way!'

Such cries punctuate the youth meetings. 'Who is it this time?' people wonder. 'Could it be my own brother or sister? Is it your friend?' A young man passes close beside you and into the corridor. His head is bent forward, he is sobbing, weighed down by the burden of sin. He had thought he was living a fairly decent life, but he had never met Christ. Now he had caught a glimpse of that love streaming towards him from the Cross and suddenly he knew his life had all been worthless up to this point. But as he confronted his sin, he also saw hope beyond it—if he could come forward and reach out to it. He must go down on his knees and confess.

Here is a girl of 17, there an older man with a grown-up family going down the corridor. He thought he had brought up a decent family, but he had concealed the name of Christ from them, denied them knowledge of that very love which should have been at the centre of their being. He will change that now.

Here is a young man whose mother showed him the way of truth when he was young. But she had died and her voice grew more distant. If only he could hear her call to him now. But suddenly—'Let him through!' Christ is at the other end to greet him with a welcome no human family ever provided. At the *mayevka* of 1973, there were at least 1,800 people present, though it was a little difficult to count, as people were still arriving when the police moved in to disrupt the meeting and try to disperse it.

There were no fewer in other years. On 1 May 1977 the youth meeting lasted from 6pm until midnight and the chill of the evening did not cool the ardour of those present. Two lads from Moscow were there, who had apparently turned up for lack of anything better to do. No one thought they were even on the wavelength of the meeting. Then suddenly one of them exclaimed, 'God forgive me my hippy life-style. I've just been a lay-about.' They came forward through the corridor and repented, joining the inner kneeling circle.

Next day they met in a back yard. The crowds were far too large for it and a neighbour volunteered his garden as well, even though it had only just been dug and sown for the spring. It reminded people of the day when a neighbour had complained at the overflow and the police moved in. One of the leaders was eventually brought to court and said, when accused of illegal evangelism, 'It was a bad day for the potato patch, but a great one for the kingdom of God.'

This time there were no such interruptions. A young girl came forward and spoke of her recent conversion with such simplicity and conviction that dozens of people were moved to repent. Grown men and women embraced each other like children. If only the whole country, the continent, the world, could witness such a 'May'—reflects the person who described it—what an effect it would have on the human race!

Those who had come forward must now be instructed in the faith, however inadequate the teaching materials available were. High summer was the time traditionally chosen, because the total immersion could then take place conveniently in the river or a lake.

On 14th August 1977 the crowds assembled by the lake. This was no hole-in-the-corner affair, conducted furtively out of sight of the authorities. As believers approached the place they were drawn and guided by the distant strains of the brass band, assembled in full force that day. As the sound grew stronger and they came into sight of it, they could hardly believe their eyes. The whole band was assembled on a makeshift raft of planks and barrels, wide enough to carry them in rows of six. It floated free in front of the crowds, guided into position by oarsmen, who still left room enough for a trumpeter to stand in front and lead them through their music. Little sails surmounted the ensemble proclaiming to the world in bold lettering, 'Believe in God'.

Dressed in shining white robes, 105 new Christians, mostly young, descended a flight of wooden steps into the lake that day. The jubilee volume shows us the very act, as the vast crowd shares their rejoicing and gives them flowers, in the knowledge that a whole new generation is now spiritually prepared to walk with Christ on the way of the Cross. Some already that day preached their first sermon and saw their first conversions as a result. But not all such great events could be crowded into the short summer months. Nor was it satisfactory from October to April to meet just in small groups at addresses that were only too easy for the KGB to observe, ready to move in, break up the meetings, arrest the leaders and confiscate the few precious books which the believers possessed.

The centenary of the Russian Bible fell in December 1976 and it would be impossible, everyone thought, to make satisfactory arrangements for the throng who would wish to celebrate this. They could not think of a place where even a fifth of them could assemble. Perhaps even there would be no general meeting at all.

A few were in on the secret, as there was much work to do in preparation. Nevertheless, the majority were quite unprepared for what met their eyes as they approached the agreed address through the uncommonly mild though very wet weather. Friends followed friends—through the door of a very ordinary house. Its door proclaimed that it was a 'Baptist Prayer House'—but how could it be? the crowds went in—and right through into the courtyard beyond. But the courtyard was almost filled by a massive structure—and you were inside it almost before you could look at it.

The 'Twentieth-Century Tabernacle' was resplendent and looked too permanent to have been erected in a few days. The new arrivals blinked and their mouths dropped open in amazement. The walls and doors were of cardboard. Transparent plastic covered the whole structure, suffusing the scene with a clear soft light. A hundred feet long, 35 across and 20 feet high, it had a pointed roof supported by poles down the middle, just like a marquee, across which stretched broad banners with sentences honouring the Bible. Facing you as you came in was a large picture of a Bible from which radiated beams of light which, in their turn, were breaking the chains of this world.

People kept on and on coming and soon the tabernacle was warm with the breath of 1,000 or more people standing shoulder to shoulder. Heartfelt prayer resounded in thanks for the gift of this place. Two old men came forward and, with great reverence, elevated a huge ancient Bible with their calloused hands, then passed it to a younger group who had come forward; they in turn passed it on to younger people still and finally, as a symbolic gesture, it went to the tiniest children. Hymns followed, interspersed with poetry specially composed for the occasion. Then people began to declare themselves as converted. No one wanted to leave, and the celebration continued all day. The tabernacle could then be packed away in preparation for another occasion.

Relations in the late 1970s were good enough between the unregistered and the registered congregation for the former sometimes to meet on the latter's premises. So it was on 7th October 1978, when the Reform Baptists gathered in a quiet and dignified way for a service in a registered church, but the KGB found out and the legality of the building they were meeting in provided not the slightest protection from thuggery. The police evicted them, packed them into lorries and dumped them deep in the countryside. They came back for meetings in private houses the very next day, which were in their turn disrupted.

This was by no means the first time the two groups had collaborated. Believers from both groups—and probably others as well—had assembled in an unimaginable crush on 20 June that same year at the registered church at 28 Yaroslavsky Street to listen to the American astronaut, James Irwin. Because of his known Christian faith and open determination to contact believers in the Soviet Union, the authorities could not bring themselves to prepare an official welcome for him. Naturally, no announcements on the radio or in the newspapers had preceded his visit. What Soviet officialdom had intended as a non-event nevertheless turned into a major witness to the faith in Kharkov, such is the power of the bush telegraph in a country where all unwelcome news is censored.

Irwin held his audience, or at least those of them who could get inside, spellbound. He was as though pulling down in one presentation all the skeins of anti-religious falsehood which Soviet propaganda had woven in and around the space programme over the previous 20 years. Yuri Gagarin, the first man in space, was reported *ad nauseam* to have said, 'I went up there and I did not see God.' Now one of America's heroes was here saying he had come to belief in God as a child and his advancement in science and exploration had never led him to doubt it. During his flight to the moon he had palpably felt God's presence and his guidance throughout the whole mission—just as he had ever since, and now most strongly, as he was able to present his beliefs to these people so far from his homeland. He presented them with photographs of himself on the moon, which they soon turned into one of the most effective anti-anti religious propaganda leaflets ever. (There is a copy in the Keston College archive.)

An Imprisoned Leader

Under what dynamic leadership has the life of the Kharkov Baptists developed so dramatically since the 1950s? We cannot attribute it to any one person, if for no other reason than that their most outstanding man was physically not there during virtually the whole of the 1960s and a good part of the 1970s as well. Boris Zdorovets received a sentence of seven years in prison followed by three years' exile in 1961, one of the very first Reform Baptist leaders to be removed after the movement emerged.

His example proves a fact which the Soviet authorities are incapable of learning—that the power of Zdorovets absent and suffering for the faith is no less galvanising than his power present. Due to his ceaseless determination in the camps, news of his unending sufferings filtered through regularly to his family and followers. A remarkable organisation of the Reform Baptists, the first group ever established in a Communist country for the systematic defence of those unjustly imprisoned, the Council of Prisoners' Relatives, began sending abroad regular information about his conditions and those of many others. They were harsh, unbelievably so when one considers that this remarkable man was also seriously physically handicapped.

When he was a child in the war, Boris Zdorovets picked up an undetonated shell which exploded and blew off his right hand, as well as severely damaging his left eye. He overcame his handicap by working hard. He studied law and acquired a knowledge of English and German, as well as being gifted musically, with a fine baritone voice and the right personality to train choirs. He found all these talents of value when he became a Christian. He did not need the state disability pension to which he was entitled and when they specially needed him the Kharkov Baptists willingly covered his expenses for full-time Christian work.

The onset of Khrushchev's new persecution when Boris had just turned 30 made the need for the talents of people such as he especially acute. Like Georgi Vins and Gennadi Kryuchkov, his exact contemporaries, he represented a new generation of people who had not had their lives blighted by the worst of Stalin's terror. They were able to bring their fresh young talents, organisational ability and, in the case of Boris Zdorovets, legal brain to the defence of a church which was under illegal attack from the regime.

His knowledge of languages and the determination to acquire theological books in them (as nothing at all was printed for evangelicals in Russian) also brought him theological ability which was far ahead of most others in his church. When, a few years later, the Soviet authorities allowed the AUCECB in Moscow to institute a theological correspondence course, he was deeply disappointed that not only were pastors of unregistered communities to be excluded, but the lucky ones were even forbidden to pass on their study materials to others.

By this first arrest and long sentence, Pastor Zdorovets (for so he was elected by his congregation) found himself excluded from the key developments in the Reform Baptist movement during its early crucial years. His deprivations would have been too much for many men who were not physically handicapped, but he surmounted them, had a slightly easier time during the final three years of exile, and returned to his congregation at Kharkov in March 1972 in full vigour, to find that it had grown and deepened in Christian experience during his absence.

His ordeal, especially after refusing constant blandishments to collaborate, had given him greater spiritual maturity as well. The love of his wife and four children gave him a stability at home which enabled him to relaunch his regular ministry with a vigour and determination which brought riches to thousands.

Nevertheless, he was only too aware of the fragility of his position. He was constantly under threat. Before his congregation he prayed:

Lord, make me worthy to suffer for you. Give me strength to remain steadfast when I think of those who have failed because of suffering, and have bypassed Golgotha because they loved the world. I forgive those who have treated me cruelly, or will do so, because they do not know what they are doing.[5]

Not much more than a year after his release, the KGB swooped on the *mayevka* of 1973, brutally arresting Boris and several other leaders, and prepared a case which came to court at the end of August and lasted 11 days. In order to uphold their fabrications, the authorities excluded all believers from the trial except his wife, and we do not know what he said during his heroic eight-hour defence speech. Naturally, this did not save him, and his sentence was three years in prison, to be followed by seven years exile.

Thus from his early thirties to his mid-fifties, Zdorovets would have had barely more than a year of liberty, totally deprived of any part in the upbringing of his children or his vocation of normal pastoral work during that time. Such are the heroes of the suffering Church, whose names are virtually unknown to the world.

He smuggled a letter out of the prison in which he wrote:

So that the whole world shall know I love Jesus, I have decided to remain silent before them, to refuse food and drink.... My whole fault lies in not having learned to lie and dissemble.... If they give you back my body, put a plain cross beside my father's grave with the inscription: 'Here Boris Zdorovets wanted to be buried, a victim of legalised illegality, for never learning to compromise his integrity.'[6]

Nevertheless, he survived threats to incriminate his wife, to have her children removed from her, assaults in the prison and spells in the punishment cell, not only to be released on time in 1976, but even to receive an amnesty after two years of exile. Now he is back home and active again.

The conclusion of *Eben-ezer*, the Kharkov Baptists' jubilee volume—based partly on a sociological survey among 1,200 people which they had the initiative to make—was that there has never been a time in the history of the Soviet Union when there has been a greater thirst for the Gospel. Great as the growth of recent years has been, it is nothing compared with what it would be had the believers been allowed even their most elementary rights to literature and open evangelism. No one who knows the Soviet religious situation well is likely to disagree.

Chapter 7

Ukrainian Uniates: A Catacomb Church

The revival and growth of a church which has no buildings, not a single parish: this is the enigma of the Ukrainian Catholic Church today. Indeed the whole country of over 40 million people is a mystery to the world at large, Russian imperialism and Soviet propaganda having submerged its identity. The Ukrainian Catholic Church is an even greater casualty, following its official liquidation in 1946. Yet it exists still, and love of it is ingrained in people's hearts, even though there are no reliable statistics to reflect its impact. Its bishops and priests have mostly retained anonymity, while its lay leadership has increasingly sought support from world opinion. Yet the world remains deaf even to the names. For every thousand who campaigned, eventually with success, for the release of Anatoli Shcharansky, there would barely be one person who knows about Iosyp Terelya.

Yet the latter has suffered even longer, and just as undeservingly. As head of the Central Committee of Ukrainian Catholics and member of the Action Group for the Defence of the Rights of Believers and the Church in Ukraine, he has now served just one year of the 12-year sentence which was imposed on him on 20th August 1985, following his arrest on 8th February that year. Then aged 42, he had already spent over 18 years of his life in labour camps and psychiatric hospitals. The appeals of his wife, Olena, have reached few of the public who listened to Avital Shcharansky. It is not even likely that a future 'exchange list' by the superpowers would include these Ukrainian names, and the vast majority of Christians in the West do not even know of the existence of the church he represents.

The story of this brave Christian will serve to illustrate the tragic fate of the largest church in the Soviet Union with no legal existence, one which has nevertheless proved that illegality and vitality can co-exist.

A Brief History

In 1596 the Commonwealth of Poland and Lithuania dominated what is now the Western Ukraine. It was here that the Ukrainian Catholic (otherwise known as the Uniate or Eastern-Rite) Church came into existence. It carried the allegiance of the majority of the faithful in that area until World War II, when it had over 4 million members. Its history is highly complex and lies generally beyond the scope of this chapter. Ukrainian Catholics worship like the Orthodox in form and language, but recognise the Pope as the head of their Church. Western Ukraine was annexed in 1939, and the church came under the Soviets, who were extremely suspicious of the allegiance of the majority of their subjects to Rome and resolved to break off contact between the Vatican and the faithful. The head of the Ukrainian Catholic Church, Metropolitan Sheptytsky, was falsely accused of being a Nazi collaborator. Following his death in 1944 his successor, Metropolitan Iosyf Slipyj, and all seven Ukrainian Catholic bishops in Western Ukraine were arrested and imprisoned; one was later murdered. The Soviet authorities unleashed a violent campaign against the Ukrainian Catholic Church, branding it in hundreds of publications as a focus of 'bourgeois nationalism' and accusing its members of collaboration with the enemy. Slipyj was

charged with hostile activities against the USSR and 'frater-
nisation with Fascists'. He and his bishops were sentenced
to between five and ten years' imprisonment, subsequently
prolonged. Only Slipyj survived, spending 17 years in concentration camps.

At the same time, with the active support of the Moscow
Patriarchate, the Soviet authorities initiated a massive campaign for the 'reunification' of the Ukrainian Catholic
Church with the Russian Orthodox Church. This take-over
occurred at the Synod of Lviv in 1946 which was attended
by some of the Catholic clergy, but without a single bishop
present. The vast majority of Ukrainian Catholics regarded
the synod as uncanonical and unrepresentative, but none
the less it sealed their fate and theoretically liquidated their
church on Soviet soil. The majority of the priests followed
the example of their bishops in refusing to embrace Orthodoxy and received similar prison sentences as a result.
About 300 Ukrainian Catholic priests managed to escape
abroad, where they and their successors maintain a vigorous ministry in many countries, especially Canada. Between 1945 and 1953 half of the 2,950 diocesan priests were
imprisoned. Others continued to operate underground.
Some died in mysterious circumstances. About 1,600
monks and nuns were expelled from their monasteries and
convents and many were imprisoned, together with hundreds of thousands of ordinary believers. The same fate
awaited 540 seminarists. All 4,440 churches and chapels
passed into Orthodox hands or were closed. More than
1,000 Catholic schools and other social institutions were
disbanded and all the 28 Catholic periodicals ceased publication.

The Ukrainian Catholic Church and the Vatican
To this day, the Ukrainian Catholic Church is consistently
persecuted by the Soviet authorities and yet it continues to
bear witness to the truth. Until the election of the Polish

Pope, John Paul II, the Ukrainian Catholics struggled to maintain the life of their 'underground' church without a great deal of visible support from the Vatican.

During the period of de-Stalinisation in the 1950s and the subsequent development of a more conciliatory policy towards the Soviet Union by the Vatican, there was no significant improvement in the lot of the Ukrainian Catholics. However, as a result of international pressure and the efforts of Pope John XXIII, Iosyf Slipyj was released from prison in Siberia in 1963 and allowed to go to Rome, where he lived until his death in September 1984 at the age of 92. In Rome he became the spiritual leader of the Ukrainian Catholic Church in the West and was made a Cardinal in 1965. He expressed constant concern for the suffering of his Church, and was not afraid to criticise the Vatican when he considered that its policy towards the Soviet Union was too conciliatory.

The Polish Pope has an automatic sympathy for the Ukrainian Catholics. At the fourth synod of bishops of the Ukrainian Catholic Church held in Rome in October 1985, the Pope renewed his plea for religious liberty and legal recognition for Ukrainian Catholics in the USSR. This type of statement by the Pope infuriates the Soviet authorities and has led to an increase of sharply worded attacks against the Vatican, as well as against Ukrainian Catholic believers, possibly even to Soviet involvement in the assassination attempt against the Pope, though this has never been proved. The Pope's relations with the Ukrainian Catholic Church in the West are regarded by the Soviet authorities as 'provocation by the Vatican' and as an attempt to 'interfere in the internal affairs of the Soviet Union'. In summer 1981 an official pamphlet entitled *The Uniate Church and Fascism* was published in Lviv. The author asserts that the present activities of Pope John Paul II are a front for the aspirations of the 'revanchists', of the enemies of democracy and of neo-fascists. In the chapter 'In the service of the neo-fascists' the author writes:

Revanchists and enemies of democracy and socialism look with
hope upon the new Pope ... for he has made it his goal to unite
Catholics all over the planet into a single anti-Communist force. It
is dictated not by anxiety for mankind and its future, but by the desire for religious authority over the planet.[1]

Clearly, the fate of the Ukrainian Catholic Church is a
matter of deep concern to the Pope and to the Ukrainian
Catholic community in exile, but should it not be a matter
of concern for Christians of all denominations throughout
the world? Apart from anything else, the Ukrainian
Catholics who are struggling so desperately for the legalisation of their church within the Soviet Union deserve a place
of honour among Christians of the world for their example
of fearless devotion to Jesus Christ in the teeth of persecution along the road to Golgotha.

Ukrainian Catholics Appeal to Fellow Believers
In January 1980 anonymous members of the Ukrainian
Catholic Church wrote a lengthy document describing
some of the great hardships which their church endures and
the suffering of many individuals and local churches in the
villages of Western Ukraine. The following passages,
slightly edited, are quoted directly from the document. It
begins by stating that no Ukrainian Catholic priest can
obtain official registration to carry out pastoral work.

However, all are 'registered' for persecution. For engaging in any
aspect of pastoral work, such as confession and burial, a priest is
fined 50 roubles every time and is threatened with a prison sentence of seven years. From time to time every priest is called to the
office of religious affairs and ordered to sign a document stating
that he will not carry out pastoral duties. Of course such a priest
will never sign, but because of this he is punished—some lose their
residence permits, some are fined or dismissed from work. All
priests who are not pensioners have to work somewhere in a gov-

ernment institution, the majority as watchmen, stokers, care-takers or odd-job men.

During searches which take place under any pretext and at any time, the militia and KGB remove literally everything that is necessary for or connected with pastoral work: prayer books, vestments, sacred objects for services of worship. After such raids it is impossible to hold a service or to perform other pastoral duties.[2]

The next section of the document describes the attempts made by Ukrainian Catholics to obtain registration and permission to use churches for worship. It refers specifically to the ongoing struggle of the villagers in Mshana, in the Lviv region.

Despite three years of constant petitioning for registration, despite several promises 'to resolve the issue positively', up until now, at the beginning of 1980, we do not have a single officially-registered holy place (church) nor even one house of prayer. We are maliciously persecuted and they have tried to make us forget everything Catholic, to force us to become atheists or, as a last resort, Russian Orthodox laity....

Over the last two to three years there has been an 'offensive' against local Catholic churches. Because believers pray there they are persecuted, the churches are turned into warehouses, closed or even destroyed.

In our village of Mshana, one day in December 1977, without any warning, four cars packed with militia and KGB agents, some of them armed and with guard dogs, came roaring up to the church. Dogs and truncheons kept believers at a distance. The church was brutally vandalised. All the altars, pulpits and seats were broken and the iconostasis was torn from the wall. Everything was taken from the church—vestments, priests' cassocks, chalices, all the church belongings, including napkins, table cloths, towels decorated with Ukrainian national embroidery and even icons. The believers appealed to the Council for Religious Affairs in Moscow. At first the delegation of believers was shouted down and beaten, then, on the second day, they were allowed to speak and were promised that the question would be considered.[3]

The villagers tried once more to register their church, but with no success. The local authorities commandeered it, first as a factory for television sets, then as a paper store.

As we have seen from the example of other religious communities in the Soviet Union, Christian education for their children is a matter of deep concern to all believing parents, and this applies equally to Ukrainian Catholics. The authors of the document describe some of the methods used in school in intimidate believers' children and to attempt to keep them away from school.

It is quite common for children as young as seven or eight years of age to be given questionnaires to fill in at school about their own and their parents' religious beliefs. The teachers dictate the 'correct' answers—that no religious beliefs are held—and the questionnaires are subsequently used as evidence that the Soviet Union is successfully educating a new generation of atheists. Special patrols of teachers or Komsomol members are posted at churches on feast days or festivals and children are either prevented from entering church or photographed and later 're-educated' at school.

Christian students face a crisis of conscience when trying to gain admission to university or any institute of higher education. Many deny their Christian beliefs in writing in order to succeed and avoid persecution, but secretly remain believers. Priests are unhappy about this course of action, but recognise that young people must have an opportunity to study and educate themselves. Those students who openly declare their beliefs are forcibly subjected to re-education. Despite the innumerable obstacles and setbacks, the authors of the document remain positive, asserting that nothing will prevent them from continuing to worship God.

Services of worship and Holy Communion are held two

or three times a month. Undoubtedly there is a special dimension present in these services, an intensity and a poignancy which is felt as a result of the persecution endured by the believers. Their spiritual needs are correspondingly met in a far deeper way than that experienced by Christians who are free to worship as they choose.

The document concludes with a further reference to the church in Mshana and an appeal for prayer:

By the closed church in the village of Mshana, where the laypeople gather for prayer in the heat of the sun or during the frosts, for the third year in succession on Christmas Eve, the Infant Jesus is born on the altar under the bare sky, just as he was in Bethlehem, bringing us Ukrainian Catholics not only his grace, but also rejoicing at the birth of Christ and strength for the victorious Resurrection. We thank all those who help us by their prayers and voices of support. May God bless you all.

Pray, brothers, Catholics of the whole world and all people of good will, that the Almighty will lessen our trials and give the church strength to endure all suffering for the glory of God and in confirmation of the words of Jesus Christ: 'The gates of Hades will not overcome it' (Matt 16:18).[4]

Iosyp Terelya Defends his Church

While many Ukrainian Catholics have remained anonymous, some have sought publicity. In 1982 Iosyp Terelya wrote a letter to a West German Catholic leader, Hans Maier, in which he indicated the role of the Church and the responsibility of believers in today's world:

The thorny path now trodden by the Ukrainian Catholic Church leads our people towards love, towards the purpose of Christianity throughout the world—the kingdom of God. International rivalry and strife should disappear in the way of unity shown in the new commands of Jesus Christ. We, Catholic Christians, cannot be passive observers of the destruction of the world.[5]

In a letter to President Reagan Terelya asks:

Can a Christian stand apart from today's events which are taking place in the modern world? When the fate of humanity is being decided, can we Christians fail to participate in the general discussion—would this not testify to our indifference to the social good?[6]

It seems axiomatic that a man serving a 12-year sentence for reasons of conscience should be recognised and heard as an authentic Christian voice, with a contribution to make to the debate on a major issue in the modern world. His fellow-Christians of all denominations should at least listen to what he has to say. To those who have come to hear his voice, he is a hero.

Terelya was born in 1943 in Hungarian-occupied Carpatho-Ukraine (now the Transcarpathian Region of the Ukrainian Republic). His parents were Communists, but when he was a child he used to go to church with his grandmother. He first got into trouble at school for fighting Russians who insulted him for being a Ukrainian. In 1962 he was sentenced to four years in a labour camp, on an allegedly criminal charge, and later received supplementary sentences for trying to escape. In 1967 he was sentenced to eight years' strict-regime camp for 'slandering' the Soviet state. He was not allowed to write any letters to his relatives from March 1966 to May 1969. In a letter which Terelya wrote in December 1976 to Yuri Andropov, then head of the KGB, he described the cruelty of the camp guards towards religious believers. He himself was made to undress and stand outside in the middle of winter, a bucket of water was thrown over him to 'baptise' him and he was mockingly given an icon to hold in order to 'save' him. Prisoners as a rule had their own crosses and icons confiscated. In 1972 he was charged with writing and disseminating Ukrainian poetry, diagnosed as mentally ill and sent to a special psychiatric hospital near Smolensk. He described this

as being run like a prison camp, with 300 political prisoners
among the genuinely insane and criminal inmates. Terelya
came across a number of political prisoners who were in
fact religious prisoners of conscience. Prisoners were completely at the mercy of the guards and subjected to humiliation and torture. Some were even killed indiscriminately by
the hospital authorities, sometimes as a reprisal, sometimes
just as a diversion. Terelya was punished for being in
possession of writing paper and was given no treatment for
his stomach and liver disorders.

In April 1976 he was released and married his fiancée
Olena, who had waited throughout the 14 years of his captivity (1962–1976). She was immediately sacked from her
job and refused a residence permit in the same town as her
husband. In August 1976 Terelya applied to a Russian
Orthodox bishop asking to be considered for the priesthood (that is, of the denomination which had officially
'absorbed' his own church). After receiving permission
from the bishop and a local representative of the Council on
Religious Affairs to study theology, he was the victim of a
sudden mysterious attack. A group of unknown men seized
him, dragged him into a car, threatened him and told him
not to go to church or spread 'religious propaganda'. He
was warned not to 'make a Jesus out of himself' and told
that 'Jesus was invented by the Jews'. He was taken to a de-
serted graveyard, tied to a cross and abandoned.

In November 1976 he was detained in another mental
hospital for two weeks, but then declared sane and released
without a warning. After he wrote to Andropov in
December the police again harassed him and eventually detained him in yet another mental hospital in April 1977. His
health deteriorated. The Soviets use a form of torture in
these hospitals by administering harmful drugs. As a result,
Terelya almost lost his capacity to read and write. They did
not leave him alone even during a few brief intervals of
freedom. His wife publicly appealed on his behalf and was
herself subjected to intimidation. Terelya has been

punished over all these years for the 'crime' of trying to defend and to obtain the legalisation of his church.

During 1982 his activities became more focussed. On 9th September he and four associates founded the Action Group for the Defence of the Rights of Believers and the Church. This was so brave it is hard for us to comprehend, when one considers that other unofficial groups formed in the Soviet Union in the 1970s to protest against the violations of the rights of other believers had just been severely repressed by the authorities, many of their most active members imprisoned (though a few were forced to emigrate), and that he himself had already endured half a lifetime of suffering. Terelya must have known what his fate would inevitably be.

He sent a declaration to the Central Committee of the Communist Party of Ukraine announcing the formation of the Action Group, setting out its aim of obtaining legalisation for the Ukrainian Catholic Church and naming his four associates. The declaration is a bold affirmation of the Christian faith.

The idea of Jesus Christ is one of the most revolutionary concepts of the last 20 centuries. 'Since we have now been justified by his blood, how much more shall we be saved from God's wrath through him' (Rom. 5:9)—and we must remember this and live accordingly. Where the blood of the Saviour is not acknowledged, there is, and can only be, destruction and death.

And although today the forces of evil are still strong, we Catholics believe and know that all evil will have its end, as it had its beginning—we live in a time of perpetual revolution. And so we follow Him who told us: 'But take heart! I have overcome the world' (John 16:33). Amen.[7]

The authorities moved swiftly against Terelya and arrested him for the sixth time on 24th December 1982. The circumstances of his arrest are described eloquently in an appeal addressed to Pope John Paul II from Yelena

Sannikova, a Russian Orthodox Christian, who has been active in helping victims of injustice in the USSR, particularly the disabled.

She herself has been the victim of harsh treatment at the hands of the Soviet authorities and is currently serving a four-year sentence in exile. Here is an example of grassroots ecumenism from a Christian whose own church has been traditionally hostile to the Ukrainian Catholic Church. Writing as an Orthodox Christian to the Pope, she first describes Terelya's character:

Iosyp Terelya is a clear example of a Catholic persecuted by the government only because he is an honourable, brave man and a true Christian, accepting any deprivation or torture in the name of good and love, and prepared to lay down his life for his friends...

He has undergone unbelievable torture, but nothing can break him. Each time he returns to freedom, he resumes his noble work—that of a Christian, a member of Christ's Church, a fighter-for truth and justice and a preacher of the word of God.[8]

Sannikova describes how, after the formation of the Action Group, the authorities made it impossible for Terelya to find work, leading eventually to his arrest on a charge of parasitism. He was prepared to accept any job, but no organisation in his home village would employ him. In November 1982 he was warned that he would be arrested for parasitism if he did not find work within a month. He was forced to leave his pregnant wife and daughter of five to look for a job in Lviv. However, at the last moment the firm which had agreed to take him on refused to do so, and he was arrested. His wife, Olena, by this time eight months pregnant, was not told where she could find her husband and it was several days before she eventually discovered him in an investigation prison in Uzhhorod.

A few weeks later Sannikova herself was contacted in connection with the case against Terelya. Late one evening intruders broke down the door of her Moscow flat. They refused to enter their names on the record of the search and spent the whole night there, confiscating a large quantity of human-rights literature, books, letters, addresses and manuscripts. The KGB similarly raided the homes of Ukrainian contacts of Terelya.

In her letter to Pope John Paul II, Sannikova goes on to express her fears for Terelya's fate:

Will he survive these trials—in poor health and with one heart attack behind him? One can say almost with certainty that spiritually he will survive; physically he will not.

Sannikova concludes her appeal by begging the Pope to use his authority to save Terelya and to support all the persecuted members of the Ukrainian Catholic Church.

Terelya's sixth sentence was to be a comparatively short one. Just after his release he wrote to his friends at Christmas 1981:

Dear Brothers and Sisters,
Another year of captivity has passed. Thank God, I again see the dear and familiar faces of friends and family, of my little children and my beloved wife. We live on earth in order to praise God and to attain eternal happiness. The praise of God is the aim of every creature on our sinful earth. And therefore I wish to remind you: beware of evil, do good deeds. In these difficult times for our church we must work ceaselessly—he who knocks at the door, to him shall it be opened. St Paul says: 'In fact, everyone who wants to live a godly life in Christ Jesus will be persecuted' (2 Tim 3:12).

The entire life of a Christian is the cross and martyrdom, if he wants to live according to the Gospel. The Holy Scripture says: 'I am sending you out like sheep among wolves' (Matt 10:16). And I beg you to remember: the Lord God does not abandon him who trusts in Him.

Christ is born!
Truly he is born![9]

During Terelya's confinement in labour camp his position as chairman of the Action Group was taken over by Vasyl Kobryn, aged 48, a convert from atheism. Under him the work continued.

In addition to the letter referred to above, announcing the formation of the Action Group, members appealed to the Ukrainian authorities, pointing out the discrepancy between the state's declared principles of freedom, equality and brotherhood and its campaign of persecution against its own people, 'simply for worshipping Christ in their own language'. The authors of the appeal suggested a procedure for the legalisation of the Ukrainian Catholic Church. They formulated their proposals under nine points. Among other things, they requested that the churches, monasteries and chapels in dioceses where the majority of believers belong to the Ukrainian Catholic Church be transferred to them; there should be permission to build their own places of worship where Catholic parishioners were in a minority compared with other believers. They also asked for Catholic seminaries to be opened in Lviv and Uzhhorod.

Apart from Terelya the secretary of the group, Fr Hryhori Budzinsky, was also singled out for attack. An article was published in the main Ukrainian newspaper vilifying him for his activities.[10] This was to be the first stage in the fabrication of a criminal record which led to his arrest in October 1984 when he was 79.

Shortly after Terelya's release from labour camp in December 1983, the campaign of harassment against the group again began to gather momentum. In March 1984 the authorities summoned Terelya and informed him that a new criminal case was being prepared. On 3rd May he wrote to the Presidium of the USSR Supreme Soviet renouncing Soviet citizenship.

The beginning of 1984 also marked a new stage in the activities of the Action Group—the publication of a clandestine information bulletin entitled *The Chronicle of the Catholic Church in Ukraine*. Up to the time of writing, nine issues of this have reached the West, in addition to a 'special issue' which was published in November 1984. This latter reported that the tenth number had been produced in Ukraine, but the manuscript had been confiscated before it could be sent to the West. Just as the *Chronicle of the Lithuanian Catholic Church* has provided, over a period of 14 years, a unique insight into the life and suffering of the Catholic Church in one corner of the Soviet Empire, so this new *Chronicle* attempts to draw the world's attention to the plight of Catholics in another whose situation is even more desperate than the Lithuanians'.

The first eight issues of the *Chronicle* reached the West at the end of 1984, and they testify to the continuing vitality of Christian faith in Ukraine. In the Transcarpathian Region, a three-year underground religious studies school is in operation, we learn. Over a period of three years, 81 priests were ordained from it. The *Chronicle* indicates that a growing number of Ukrainian Catholics have been driven to the limits of civil disobedience. During the first half of 1984, over 900 believers surrendered their identity documents and refused to have any further dealings with the authorities. Terelya has predicted that if this trend continues, over 3,000 Catholics will destroy their documents. He declared in the first issue:

We are persecuted and without rights. They have taken away everything from us: our church, our educational institutions. They persecute us constantly. For the government we exist only as a work force in the concentration camps. So why do we need Soviet passports? They can put people in Soviet concentration camps without passports.[11]

The *Chronicle* does not concern itself exclusively with the Ukrainian Catholic Church, but provides information on believers of various other denominations also. This is a testimony to a growing ecumenical spirit among believers in Ukraine.

Despite the considerable risks involved in producing

samizdat publications, the appearance of the *Chronicle* has had a considerable impact which has led to the founding of other clandestine journals. The first issue of the *Ukrainian Catholic Herald* appeared in April 1984, the theme and contents being closely related to the *Chronicle*. This was followed by the appearance in 1985 of another journal, *The Independent*, which reached the West in October 1985. The first issue, consisting of eight typewritten pages, included several items concerning Ukrainian Catholic believers, among them an excerpt from the writings of the late Cardinal Slipyj, the text of a letter from Iosyp Terelya to Lech Walesa, and a report on the formation and goals of the Committee for the Defence of the Rights of Believers and the Church.

Information which appeared in both the *Chronicle* and the *Ukrainian Catholic Herald* indicates that the Soviet authorities did offer, in 1984, to legalise the Ukrainian Catholic Church, but only as an independent church with no ties to Rome. This offer was clearly not acceptable, as breaking with the Vatican would amount to renouncing Catholicism. The sixth issue of the *Chronicle* contains a reconstruction of conversations, evidently compiled from memory by Terelya, which took place on 23rd and 24th April 1984 with government representatives. In response to their demands that he register his church with the authorities, Terelya pointed out one advantage of illegal status: 'At the moment the Ukrainian Catholic Church is not under your control and we make the decisions concerning our own matters.... I do want legalisation, but not the kind that you are offering.[12]

Naturally Terelya's scepticism is born out of his knowledge of what has happened within legally-registered denominations where the Soviet government exercises rigid control and tries to reduce religious practice to worship within the four walls of a church.

Despite these apparent overtures on the part of the authorities during April, the true nature of the Communist

Party's intentions became clear in a secret decree of 3rd July 1984, referred to in the *Chronicle*, from a regional committee of the Communist Party of Ukraine, entitled 'The Improvement of Methods of Combating Manifestations of Nationalism and Zionism'. The 'manifestations' refer to the activity of religious groups. The decree notes the failure of militant atheistic education for young people, describes it as 'ineffective', but draws attention to the KGB's success in the Irshava district, where underground Baptist and Catholic printing presses have been liquidated and hundreds of copies of religious publications confiscated. Among the propositions in the document are the following: the repentance of former anti-Soviet clerics should be turned to the party's advantage by creating antinationalistic press propaganda; it is desirable that two-thirds of Catholic activists be directed for compulsory psychiatric treatment; efforts to discredit the church and its members should be made, especially in areas where the church's influence is still strong, such as the villages, but the party should avoid direct confiscation of religious objects; Sunday masses on state farms can be forbidden under the pretext of the summer season.

In 1984 the authorities struck a major blow against the Action Group: they arrested Vasyl Kobryn. It was from him that the tenth issue of the *Chronicle* was confiscated. Terelya went into hiding, where he remained for 11 weeks. According to one of his letters (dated February 1985) from prison, Terelya somehow 'surfaced' in January to negotiate with the KGB for the release of various Soviet prisoners of conscience (including Shcharansky), but no agreement was reached. He subsequently fell seriously ill and had to enter a hospital in Lviv where he was arrested, on 8th February, with a temperature of 102°. Terelya was held under investigation until his trial in August. Vasyl Kobryn was tried in March and sentenced to three years' ordinary-regime camp under the article condemning dissemination of deliberate falsehoods defaming the Soviet state and the social system.

Father Budzinsky was called as a witness at Kobryn's trial and testified to his honest character. An article in the Lviv newspaper which reported the trial noted that 'for humanitarian considerations, taking into account his advanced age', there would be no criminal charges against the octogenarian Fr Budzinsky.[13]

Terelya was sentenced on 20th August to seven years in labour camps, followed by five years' exile, for 'anti-Soviet agitation and propaganda'. Among the grounds for his conviction were the letter quoted above to Hans Maier, his renunciation of Soviet citizenship, his dissemination of 'anti-Soviet literature', and his co-publication of the *Chronicle of the Catholic Church in Ukraine*.

In his final statement Terelya declared himself not guilty of the charges, pointing out that freedom of religion and conscience were guaranteed by the Soviet Constitution. In the verdict the judge emphasised that the 12-year sentence should serve as an example to those 'who had not grasped the seriousness of the situation'.

After his trial Terelya was sent to Camp No 36–1 near Kuchino in the Perm Region of Russia. Several renowned prisoners of conscience have been confined to this area, including Anatoli Shcharansky. Within a period of 16 months (May 1984–September 1985) four Ukrainian prisoners of conscience confined in Camp No 36—three who had set up human rights groups for monitoring the Helsinki Agreement, and the Ukrainian Catholic, Valeri Marchenko—died, three of them due to medical neglect by the camp authorities. Camp 36 is commonly known as a death-camp.

Olena was urged by the authorities to divorce her husband, but refused. She had already experienced an even longer agony of waiting for a loved one than Avital Shcharansky: her separation from Terelya while he was in prison during their engagement lasted 14 years. Now she faces another long period of isolation from her husband, and her children will grow up fatherless. She has been unable to find work and has to endure conditions of poverty (as there are no welfare benefits for prisoners' relatives in the USSR).

It is fitting to end this chapter by quoting a further extract from Terelya's letter to the Central Committee of the Communist Party of Ukraine, written in September 1982. Perhaps in this letter he foretells his own destiny:

Despite the declaration and prognoses of some party members, we are living, growing and triumphing. The trials and persecutions suffered by Catholics in Ukraine have strengthened us even more in the faith, and have given us the opportunity to sound the depths of God's providence. I can state without exaggeration that there is nothing greater than to die a Catholic in a Communist prison. He who loses fear gains truth and hope. That is why we believe that the Kingdom of God is coming, and shall have no end.[14]

Chapter 8

Lithuanian Catholics: Stronghold under Siege

In 1969 a lecturer at the Medical School in Klaipeda, a busy seaport on the Baltic Coast of Lithuania, was marking examination papers submitted by his 19-year old students. He had given a compulsory course on atheism and the students had to come up with the correct 'ideological' answers in order to pass and move on to the next phase of their training. He was astonished to read the following answer submitted by a female student:

It has been asserted that the various religions originated from human helplessness and ignorance, but this is not true. The origin of religion is much more sublime.... Scientists discover various scientific principles. Doesn't this lead man to question that some higher being must have laid down these principles? Man is more than a hunk of meat and a pile of bones: he has an immortal soul. Christ really lived and the calendar is calculated from the time of his birth.... Life would be ideal and beautiful, even heaven-like, if all men were true and loyal Catholics. No army, police or prisons would be needed, but now.... I think the Catholic faith is correct. I have been of that opinion for a long time; the atheism courses have served only to confirm my thinking.[1]

We know about this particular incident because it was recorded in the pages of a remarkable journal entitled the

Chronicle of the Lithuanian Catholic Church, which has been secretly produced and distributed in Lithuania since 1972. Copies that regularly reach the West form the main source of information about the life of the Catholic Church in Lithuania today.

Who was this courageous student who dared to write in defence of Christianity, knowing that the consequences would be unpleasant—reprimands, ridicule, threats and possible expulsion from the medical school—thus jeopardising her whole career? The *Chronicle* does not name her, but for the purposes of this chapter about the church in Klaipeda and the Catholic faith in Lithuania as a whole, we will call her Vanda and try to discover what influenced her in her search for truth and led her to the Christian faith.

Vanda was born in 1950. Her parents were devout Catholics who taught their daughter the Christian faith almost from the cradle. They had lived through some of the most difficult and tragic years of Lithuania's history, a country once briefly independent, like Estonia, and now, by force of military might, incorporated into the Soviet Union. Their love for their country with its distinctive culture, language and traditions, was inseparably bound up with their love for God and the Catholic Church and it was their faith which had sustained them during the war years and as they faced the future. The prospect of seeing their country further 'sovietised'—and already they had witnessed the destruction wrought in all walks of life by the implantation of an alien, materialistic, atheist ideology—filled them with dismay. They felt powerless. But the birth of their daughter brought them not only great joy, but also a determination to preserve all that they could of their Lithuanian way of life within the family and to bring her up to love God and her country and to develop a keen awareness of its history.

A Victim of Geography

Lithuania is the most southerly of the three Baltic States. In contrast to Latvia and Estonia, traditionally strongholds of the Lutheran faith, it has always been close to Poland, the birthplace of the present Pope and centre of spiritual revival of the Catholic Church. Lithuanians were subjected to years of autocratic rule by the Russian tsars but retained the Catholic faith, despite attempts to convert them to the Orthodox Church of Russia.

As in the other Baltic States, the Russian Revolution of 1917 gave Lithuania the opportunity to regain national independence. The Molotov-Ribbentrop Pact of August 1939 brought that independence to an end by awarding the Baltic States and part of Poland to the Soviet Union in return for German possession of the rest of Poland and a free hand in Western Europe. Soviet troops invaded Lithuania in July 1940. The Soviets immediately established their 'legitimacy' in this newly conquered territory by organising an election in which all the candidates were Communist Party members or affiliated to Communist Party organisations. All other political parties and organisations had been banned.

As in Estonia (see p 22), local people were ousted from positions of power and influence in society. There were mass deportations to Siberia, Kazakhstan or Central Asia. Among the categories of Lithuanians being deported for 'hostility to the new regime' were clergy of all denominations.

The exiles included many sick, elderly people and young children. Nowhere did the faith do more to hold the Lithuanian people together than during the deportation. Dmitri Panin, a former companion of Solzhenitsyn in the camps, describes the Lithuanians' daily evening prayer:

They knelt facing the wall, crossed themselves and prayed for five to ten minutes. Before long we came to imitate them, because the example they gave us made us blush with shame at not having the bravery to bear witness to our faith. Moreover, these brave country folk openly wore their baptismal crosses on their necks, thus making a silent testimony to their belonging to Jesus Christ.[2]

A tiny proportion of these captives eventually returned to their homeland but were never able to enjoy the Lithuania they had once known, for the process of sovietisation had begun.

It soon became obvious that the separation of church and state, the constitutional principle of Soviet religious policy, was to mean the abolition of the power of the church and control by the state. The authority of the Lithuanian Catholic Church was transmitted from Rome and so, as a first step, the Soviet administration severed diplomatic links with the Vatican. Not only were all state subsidies abolished, but all church property was confiscated, as were pension funds, the savings of individual clergy and the bank accounts of parishes and all religious organisations. Only a skeletal structure of central church administration was allowed to continue.

The Catholic Church has always encouraged a wealth of activities outside the confines of worship, particularly in the realm of education and charitable work. Thus the annihilation of all Catholic societies and organisations and the confiscation of their assets was a devastating blow to the influence of the church. All specialised activities became illegal. Religious orders were banned. Monasteries and convents were totally abolished. All chaplaincy work in the army, prisons, schools, hospitals and old people's homes came to an end. There were bureaucratic new regulations which made the simplest task of ordinary parish priests, such as visiting the sick and dying, extremely difficult.

Religious publishing houses were taken over and their assets nationalised. Thus the publication of all religious newspapers, books and journals came to an end. Libraries, monasteries, schools and archives had to surrender all religious books, which were then burned. Secular newspapers which, during the period of Lithuania's independence, had always given space to the discussion of religious topics, had to replace such discussion with crude anti-religious propaganda.

Wayside crosses and shrines had always been a prominent feature of Christian Lithuania. They were visible everywhere—on the walls of hospitals and schools and in private gardens. These were desecrated and demolished and replaced by red stars and other symbols of Soviet power. Religious holidays were abolished, including All Saints' Day, All Souls' Day and Christmas. All religious street processions, such an important part of the public witness of the Catholic Church in Lithuania, were banned.

There were other systematic attempts to subvert the power of the church. District chiefs of the NKVD (secret police) were instructed to keep a close watch on all bishops and clergy and to enlist priests and suitable laymen as spies so that dossiers could be compiled detailing all the continuing activities and contacts of the faithful.

The government imposed an obligation on all clergy to be loyal to the Soviet State that involved signing a declaration. This immediately gave rise to a crisis of conscience, for how could a priest declare his loyalty to an atheist state bent on eradicating religious belief from society?

All this happened in a period of 12 months before the Nazi invasion of the Soviet Union curtailed, temporarily, this ruthless attack on the church. Despite all these pressures, the mass of believers and clergy stood firm in their allegiance to the Christian faith and the church. But the psychological damage inflicted by this crude and heartless campaign against all that the Lithuanian people held dear gave rise to a hostility and mistrust of the Soviet rulers which persists to this day. This outline is also a microcosm of Soviet policy towards religion.

When the Nazis invaded the Soviet Union in June 1941

the Lithuanians immediately and spontaneously revolted against their Soviet overlords and established a Provisional Government for six weeks before it was suppressed by the German invaders.

Lithuania had no breathing space between the retreat of the Germans and the reoccupation of their land by the Red Army. During the years 1944–1953 over 200,000 more Lithuanians were deported to various 'islands' of the Gulag Archipelago. Following Stalin's death in March 1953, some of those who had been exiled were allowed to return, but they constituted only a tenth of the number originally deported.

Building a Church

Vanda's parents, engaged to be married at the time, were both living in Klaipeda when the war was coming to an end in 1945. They had vivid memories of one particular day when Hitler's army mined and destroyed the brick Catholic Church. The faithful were stunned by this act of violent desecration, and once the Germans had fled they appealed to their Soviet rulers to provide an alternative building in which they could worship. At first the congregation was told it could share the premises of the small church belonging to German Baptists, but the services became so overcrowded that people regularly fainted and the Catholics requested permission to build a larger church. To everyone's amazement, in 1954 Fr (now Bishop) Liudas Povilonis, the pastor of Klaipeda, received permission to build a new church. A wave of joy and optimism spread through the Catholic community and everyone began to think about what he or she could contribute to the project. Vanda's grandfather, a skilled stone mason, immediately began to draw designs for an altar frieze depicting the Last Supper, and her grandmother somehow managed to obtain fine linen on which to embroider a traditional Lithuanian motif to be used as an altar cloth. A detailed account of the building of the church, written in 1972, was published in the pages of the *Chronicle*. The scepticism which local people felt about the motives of the government in allowing the church to be built did not diminish their enthusiasm in setting about the task. The authors of the account stated that permission was granted for propaganda purposes because Klaipeda is a busy port visited by many foreign seamen. Apparently government representatives told the congregation: 'Build it so that the steeple can be seen from the sea'. At the time there was a great shortage of construction materials, but the government even permitted building reserves to be used for the construction of the church. On 30th June 1957 Bishop Petras Maželis blessed the foundation of the new church and a document recording the event was placed in the foundations. Vanda, then aged seven, was an onlooker at this solemn occasion. The *Chronicle* describes the building project.

Offerings were collected throughout Lithuania for the construction of the church. The Catholics of Klaipeda joined in the enterprise with joy and enthusiasm. Even though the site was very boggy, within a few weeks the people had filled in the marsh, using small carts and even baskets of earth. After returning home from work, believers hurried to help in the construction and worked late into the night. Drivers brought the necessary materials in their own time and collected bricks among the ruins in the city. Even inspectors turned a blind eye as drivers helped in the work and some officials would come to help the believers. Among the helpers were people who had never previously been to church.

The believers collected about three million roubles for the church building fund. Even poor Catholics gave joyfully of their savings. One worker who brought a considerable sum of money said, 'Put my heart among the bricks in the walls of the church'. It turned out that this man, who had a large family to support, had contributed one month's wages. When people sold anything, they allocated part of the money for the church. The church was completed during the summer of 1960 and the consecration ceremonies were to be held on the Feast of the Assumption.[3]

But the consecration ceremony never took place. The Government of the Lithuanian Republic issued an order forbidding the opening of the church. This event was, of course, a reflection of the new wave of intense persecution of the Church that swept through the Soviet Union under Khrushchev. The resulting anguish for the Catholics of Klaipeda is described vividly in the *Chronicle*.

The atheists acted in total disregard of people's feelings. During the night the army knocked down the church steeple with tractors. They defaced the stations of the Cross and threw them into the mud. The people's only defence against the whims of the army and police was tears. Policemen hunted them down and took them into custody. Others were taken by lorries 40 or 50 kilometres out of town and told to walk home. Such harsh conduct towards the church and believers is unimaginable in any nation which respects basic human rights. The believers, by whose contributions and physical exertions the church was built, were bitterly wounded.

'This is the true face of an ungodly government,' said the people through their tears. 'We must complain to higher authority...'

'To whom can we complain when believers are considered to be outside the law? The godless government won't defend our rights.'

The government, fearing a riot by the believers, sent in about 200 police.

At the beginning of 1961 two priests of Klaipeda, Frs Povilonis and Burneikis, were arrested and sentenced to prison. Father Talaisis was exiled from Klaipeda.

At present the new church in Klaipeda is used as a public concert hall. At first no people holding religious beliefs, whether Lithuanians or Russians, would go to the concerts. There were times when 50 artists performed on stage but there were only five in the audience.[4]

The Klaipeda congregation has no church to this day. They have to make do as best they can using a small chapel of 290 square metres. The population of Kaipeda has increased enormously since the church was built, and with it the number of Catholics. Fortunately, the congregation does not depend on a building in order to keep its faith alive and maintain its witness, but the lack of any adequate meeting place restricts its activities.

Undoubtedly one of the many factors that has maintained the unity and witness of the Klaipeda church is the struggle by its members to win back their church from the Soviet authorities. In this they have been joined by thousands of Catholics from all over Lithuania who have identified themselves with the Klaipeda Catholics through prayer and the signing of numerous petitions to a succession of Soviet leaders.

During 1979 over 148,000 signatures were gathered throughout the country and attached to an appeal addressed to Leonid Brezhnev demanding the return of the Klaipeda church. The believers gave a detailed account of the building of the church and its subsequent desecration, pointing out that the whole episode was a blot on the reputation of the Soviet government in the eyes of the world. They vowed to continue with their protests and petitions until the church was returned. They have not given up, but with no result so far. The most recent report in the *Chronicle* concerning the Klaipeda church gives details of a petition dated January 1983 addressed to Yuri Andropov and bearing 22,500 signatures. No doubt Mr Gorbachov will be the recipient of similar documents from the Catholics of Lithuania.

For many young people like Vanda, who grew up in Klaipeda under the influence of Christian parents and grandparents who were personally so closely involved with the building of the church, the incident has had a most profound effect. Young people educated entirely within the Soviet system with its emphasis on a materialistic world

view and atheist indoctrination continue to be loyal to the
church, even to the point of risking their future careers.
Often the awareness of a deep divide between the Marxist
theory of an equal and just society and what they see being
worked out in their daily lives stimulates them to search for
an alternative ideology. Many of them thus turn to the
Christian faith. Vanda, now in her mid-thirties, and probably bringing up her own family, is likely to be as staunchly
Catholic as her own parents. She and others who are involved in the struggle to win back the church in the 1980s
are the children and grandchildren of the original builders
of the church. Some of the men who dug the trenches and
carried the bricks are now pensioners. Their story could be
placed alongside that of Nehemiah who was determined,
despite seemingly impossible odds, to rebuild the walls of
the Holy City of Jerusalem. The Klaipeda Catholics are
bound to succeed eventually.

The events in Klaipeda had particularly far-reaching
effects for the local pastor, Fr Povilonis. He was accused of
illegally acquiring building materials and sentenced to eight
years in prison, but he received an amnesty after serving
four of them.

After his return from camp he became assistant of the
Vilnius parish of Maria Immaculata, soon becoming au-
xiliary bishop of Telšiai, then Kaunas, eventually becoming
bishop there. In some of the early issues of the *Chronicle* he
is portrayed as a leader of the church who enjoyed tre-
mendous popularity among the faithful. People flocked to
hear his sermons. In more recent years he has been the
object of criticism by the faithful for some of the things he
is reported to have said while abroad on official delegations
about the situation of the Lithuanian Church, and for not
standing up to the atheist authorities as vigorously as
people hoped he would.

In January 1980 Bishop Povilonis had to attend a briefing
in the capital, Vilnius, at the offices of the Council on
Religious Affairs. Government officials rounded upon the

bishops who were forced to attend for their part in failing to curb or even for encouraging 'extremist tendencies' among the clergy and the faithful. They were asked why it was necessary to provoke people and collect signatures for the return of the Klaipeda church. One official stated: 'The Catholics already have a church, let them pray there.' It was obvious that they had no intention of returning the confiscated church. Bishop Povilonis was singled out for criticism by the officials, who accused him of hiding behind Bishop Labukas and not speaking out more actively in criticism of believers. The mere mention of the church at Klaipeda by government officials must have come as a chilling reminder to the bishop of the most difficult and painful four years of his life. Even if this man has weakened under enormous pressures since he took on the heavy burden of high office in the Catholic Church, his earlier sacrifice should never be forgotten. During the period of his imprisonment his example clearly inspired the dispirited members of his flock.

It would be doing the Catholics of Lithuania an injustice to leave their story there, and it might give the misleading impression that their whole lives are bound up with appealing to the authorities and signing petitions. Despite the many difficulties they encounter and the petty harassment to which they are constantly subjected, they maintain their witness to the Christian faith and demonstrate their steadfastness in a whole variety of ways.

Inner Life
One of the enduring features of the life of the Christian Church which the Soviet regime has tried to erase is the Christian calendar which gives such colour and character to the succession of seasons. As we have seen with Estonia, the Soviet authorities have tried every means to replace Christian rites and festivals with secular ones. Despite all the pressures, the faithful perpetuate their traditions.

Nowhere is this more evident than in the way they continue to demand the association of the church with the most solemn moments of their personal lives: birth, coming of age, marriage, death. It is debatable whether Communism has succeeded at all in lessening this adherence, despite its claims to have done so.

The great festivals are occasions on which the church most notably crosses the frontier into secular society and bears public witness. Lithuania has a lively tradition of religious processions, both for celebration and for mourning, which naturally take place outside the church building and are therefore an increasing cause of conflict with the authorities, especially when children take part. The authorities often try to force priests themselves to forbid these traditional ways of marking allegiance to Christianity and they fine people who organise processions.

Everywhere in Lithuania the churches continue to attract huge crowds of worshippers. There is no evidence of falling away, except in the pages of atheist propaganda. In July 1973, Bishop Povilonis visited the parish of Viesiejai for a confirmation. Altogether 2,600 candidates and 10,100 people were present, of whom over a third received communion. The *Lithuanian Chronicle* refers many times to large numbers of people often overflowing the inadequate facilities for worship. Those who usually attend church are not passive or curious onlookers. Vast numbers of people make their confession, and the *Chronicle* sometimes describes the priest as being besieged by crowds of people.

In addition to church-going, the faithful express their Christian commitment by making pilgrimages to national shrines. The widespread devotion to the Cross in Lithuania begins in people's own homes and continues outside. There is an old tradition that individuals should erect crosses in the immediate surroundings of their own houses and this has led, not surprisingly, to an endless series of clashes with the authorities.

One of the greatest national shrines is at Šiluva, where

week-long devotions on the Nativity of the Blessed Virgin Mary in early September traditionally attract huge crowds from all over Lithuania. The authorities do their best to disrupt the proceedings by holding back buses and cars and setting up road blocks, so that even very elderly people have to walk for miles to reach the town itself. In 1983, according to the *Chronicle*, roughly 50,000 pilgrims participated in the religious festival at Šiluva, of whom 40,000 people received Communion.

One of the most remarkable places of popular devotion in Lithuania is the Hill of Crosses near Šiauliai. The origin of the shrine dates back to 1861 when Lithuanians began an uprising against the Russians. A small chapel once stood at the foot of a hill near Šiauliai where Lithuanian insurgents gathered to pray. Cossack soldiers locked the doors of the chapel and buried it with the men inside, completely covering it with earth. In time the roof of the chapel rotted away and caved in, which is why the hill today has a hollow in the middle. At first people put up crosses on the hill in honour of the revolutionaries, but later they put them there as petitions or acts of thanksgiving to God. At one time there were 3,000 large crosses and countless smaller ones, each with its own history. One Lithuanian priest wrote about the hill as follows:

Many people used to come on foot carrying the crosses to erect them. Several of them had been brought from Latvia, Estonia, Belorussia and even from America. People say, 'How much suffering, how many illnesses we have brought to this hill. One wonders how the mound can bear all the trouble. It's a real Lithuanian Golgotha.'[5]

The Hill of Crosses was razed to the ground during the Khrushchev persecution. Gradually the site was 'replanted' with crosses and then again totally devastated by the authorities in 1973. The erection of crosses by believers and their removal by the authorities continues to this day. One author wrote about a scene he observed there in October

1975.

At 8am a bus arrived at the hill and a large group of young
people—university students and senior schoolchildren—swarmed
out. The young people took a cross from inside the bus and together they put it at the foot of the hill. The girls then decorated
it with flowers of rue. They all then carried it up the hill, each trying to play his part in bearing the noble burden. Candles were lit
around the cross after its erection and all knelt in prayer:

'Lord, give us the strength to confess our faith courageously and
to show that we love you!

'Lord, help us to conquer the present evils of our nation: lack of
faith, immorality and drunkenness!

'Lord, help the young people of Lithuania, both of our own
town and of the whole nation!

'Lord, be merciful to those who with blasphemous hands
destroy the crosses we erect and desecrate Lithuania's holy
place.'[6]

Given the popular devotion especially of the young to
this holy shrine, it is hardly surprising that the authorities
continue to do everything in their power to disrupt pilgrimages and inconvenience the pilgrims, but it seems that nothing can deter the faithful.

The Hill of Crosses has become a symbol of hope for
Lithuanian Catholics in their struggle against an atheist
regime. In 1977 another pilgrim wrote the following:

The authorities have not succeeded and will not succeed in rooting
out the faith from the hearts of the people. Alongside the black-
ened tree trunk of a maple, planted during Lithuania's independence and cut down during the last atheist desecration, a large and
beautiful cross with a metal depiction of the torment of Christ has
again 'grown up'. It is apparently made from the same felled
maple found at the foot of the hill. It has the inscription: '2nd May
1977'. So it is regulated by God: if the roots remain the tree will
shoot up again. Atheists are helpless here![7]

Leadership

This chapter cannot be closed without mentioning two of the church's outstanding spiritual leaders, without whom it would be infinitely poorer.

Lithuanian believers depend to a great extent on their priests and bishops as a source of enlightenment, comfort and inspiration. If their spiritual leaders are in difficulties, the faithful support them through prayer and by vigorously defending them through letters and protests to the authorities. The treatment of two Catholic priests, Frs Sigitas Tamkevičius and Alfonsas Svarinskas, who have been arrested and imprisoned in recent years, provides a poignant example of how ordinary believers rally to support their priests. Fr Svarinskas was one of the founders of the Catholic Committee for the Defence of Believers' Rights, a group formed in 1978 to document and protect violations of religious liberty in Lithuania. The founding of the committee was inspired partly by the example of other similar groups, in particular the one set up by the Russian Orthodox priest Fr Gleb Yakunin in Moscow in 1976, and partly by the election of Pope John Paul II. Since its inception the Catholic Committee has issued over 50 documents, but with two of its members now in prison the work of the committee has to be continued anonymously.

Fr Svarinskas had been singled out for persecution by the Soviet authorities long before his involvement with the Catholic Committee. Prior to his arrest in January 1983 he had already served a total of 16 years in labour camps for 'anti-Soviet activities'. He was ordained priest while in a camp in 1950 and gained a reputation there for being dedicated to helping sick prisoners. His role as a member of the Catholic Committee enraged the authorities and an intense campaign in the press and on TV, in which he was singled out for attack as an 'extremist priest', preceded his eventual arrest. By the time his trial began three months later about 55,000 people had written to the authorities demanding his

release. He was sentenced in May 1983 to seven years'
strict-regime camp and three years' internal exile on
charges of slandering the Soviet state.

Fr Svarinskas wrote a personal account of his trial which
reached the West in a letter dated 8th June 1983. At the end
of it he appealed to fellow-believers in Lithuania and
throughout the world:

God has provided for me the fate of the martyrs. Therefore, it
only remains for me to show myself worthy of the grace of God.
These ten years of want and suffering will be the crown of my
priesthood. Let us pray for one another, so that we do not crumble
under the cross of the Lord.[8]

A similar fate befell Fr Tamkevičius, also a member of
the Catholic Committee for the Defence of Believers'
Rights. His trial took place in late 1983. He was charged
with anti-Soviet agitation and his list of crimes, which were
read out in court, included aiding prisoners, preaching sermons with criminal content, organising processions to
cemeteries, teaching groups of children and gathering
people around a Christmas tree. The Soviet regime has
tried to repaganise the Christmas tree as a New-Year custom, and his 'crime' here seems to have been to restore it to
its old position, thus—in the eyes of Soviet officials—up-
staging the later local New-Year tree. He was sentenced to
six years in strict-regime labour camp and four years of internal exile. In his final statement to the court, Fr
Tamkevičius described how a Soviet official had once called
him an 'adventurer who has been doing well for a long
time'. He then said the following:

No, I am not an adventurer. I am a pupil of Christ, a priest who
loves God and the people, old and young, especially young
people: to them I have dedicated my life and will later sacrifice it
if necessary. I have worked wherever God sent me and now He is
sending me where I am most needed. Today He is merely transferring me from one place to another. I have tried to accept all cross-

es given me by God and so now I take this cross, embrace and kiss it. Glory be to Jesus Christ and to Mary the blessed.[9]

No wonder the faithful of Lithuania love priests such as these. In June 1983, a month after the arrest of Fr Tamkevičius, his parishioners went around the church in procession on their knees praying for their beloved pastor.

Both priests continue to inspire the devotion of people like Vanda and her children in their turn, of their parishioners and of all believers in Lithuania through the letters they write from camp, which have been published in the *Chronicle* and circulated throughout the country. They are wonderfully moving testimonies to the triumph of faith in the midst of suffering.

In October 1984 Keston College reported that Fr Tamkevičius was working in the kitchen of a strict-regime camp in Perm Region in Siberia. Here, in conclusion, are some extracts from letters he wrote from there.

I am convinced that the work I am doing is no less necessary to the church and the believers than all I have been doing for the past 20 years.... At work I lack nothing, so in my thoughts I can be constantly with the good Lord, for in him I am also with those who were close to my heart when I was at liberty.

He asks his friends to remember him in their prayers,

that there may not be a single empty day in my working life. It would be tragic if I could not find meaning in my work. I would be like the man who buried his talent in the ground...

In the last ten months I have learned to trust God much more. Even when we forget Him, He is standing in the boat of our life and will not let it sink.

On the anniversary of his consecration as a priest, Fr Tamkevičius wrote:

18th April was a very precious day to me—the day when I would thank the Almighty for the gift of the priesthood. Twenty-two years ago, on the Wednesday before Easter (just like this year), ten deacons approached the high altar of the cathedral with trembling hearts; falling to the ground we prayed...

Then the Bishop of Telšiai, Petras Mazelis, ordained us as priests. On 23rd April (Easter Monday), I celebrated my first mass in my native parish church. I am endlessly grateful to God both for the priesthood and for the road I have travelled. I have continually felt the caring hand of Providence...

Easter has brought me much joy. Wherever you might be, the Christ who overcame death touches and revives you.... I remember those dear Easter mornings when I used to take the monstrance from Christ's tomb and intone, 'A joyful day has dawned' and a crowd of thousands, like angel choirs, would start to sing joyfully the holy Easter hymn with its 'Alleluia' of deepest beauty.... We need to sing the resurrection hymn over the years not only with our lips but with our whole lives.[10]

Chapter 9

Siberian Orthodox: Light in a Great Land

More than a few points of Christian light shine out from the vastness of the Siberian wilderness, dark in history as a land of paganism until the nineteenth century, dark physically for long stretches in the winter when the arctic sun can scarcely struggle above the horizon, dark for humanity as a place of banishment and slave labour under the Tsars and then the Soviets. Yet Siberia has also great natural beauty, both in winter and especially in summer, instantly felt by all those who visit it for the first time. Many who were born there would never live anywhere else and today some of the most intense Christian activity in the Soviet Union takes place there.

Gradually the Russians colonised this vast land from the end of the sixteenth century on, a process not completed until the construction of the last link of the Trans-Siberian Railway, 4,500 miles long, in 1917. The imposition of political centralisation and cultural uniformity could not, in many outlying areas, do more than brush the surface; only along the thread of the railway did a recognisably Russian civilisation develop. Away from this a bewildering variety of tribes, with their individual languages and customs, continued their traditional pursuits, gleaning a subsistence from reindeer herd and forest.

With the expanding use of exile as a political punishment, begun by Peter the Great in the eighteenth century,
and forced labour as a means of developing Siberia
economically, now used in the Soviet period, the religious
scene became increasingly varied. First came the Russian
sects of the Old Believers who were victims of the religious
struggles of the seventeenth century, followed later by both
Catholics and Protestants in growing numbers, many of
them non-Russians. But the great towns, Omsk,
Novosibirsk, Tomsk and Irkutsk, extended along the railway, became part of the heartland of Russian Orthodoxy,
administrative centres from which radiated an evangelistic
activity which belies the popular perception of Orthodoxy
as not being missionary-minded.

Today a visit to the great city of Irkutsk gives the impression, give or take the presence of a fair number of Asiatic
faces from the neighbouring Buryat-Mongol area, of being
almost more Russian than Moscow. The missionary tradition is still very much alive, and there are young Orthodox
priests, even today, who pray for direction to work in these
areas so that they may bring the Gospel to the Buddhist
Buryats and the pagan tribes of the Chukchi and the
Ostyaks.

Parish Life

In some ways, and especially among the young, Russian
Orthodoxy has become increasingly evangelical in recent
years. It has continued to be a traditional refuge for millions, especially the middle-aged, the elderly and the less
educated, but it has drawn in increasing numbers of the
young and of intellectuals, often only half visibly, because
of necessity they have to veil their allegiance from the eyes
of the authorities.

In contrast to Protestants and Catholics, the Orthodox
have been somewhat reticent about chronicling details of
their lives for the world at large (though we know a very

great deal more than we did 30 years ago, thanks to the activities of such groups as Fr Gleb Yakunin's Christian Committee for the Defence of Believers' Rights; and now—putting all of this into readily accessible form—Jane Ellis's comprehensive book, *The Russian Orthodox Church: A Contemporary History*.)[1] No one parish, therefore, supplies us with all the information we need about their spiritual and physical regeneration. What follows is a composite picture, of which every element is true and many times repeated, though not all aspects are present in full at the same time in the same place, and individual details are culled from a number of sources.

Near Novosibirsk in the Siberian Parish of Fr Alexander Pivovarov, Novokuznetsk, the one open Orthodox church provides a haven of joy, colour and spiritual refreshment for the local believers. The church is crowded for the main services on Saturday evenings and Sundays. Even on weekdays a good number of people come, while on major festivals, especially Easter, you have to arrive hours before the service begins in order to be assured of a place within the church at all. Full churches do illustrate the vigour of the Orthodox faith coming up to 70 years after the Revolution which brought in atheism as the basis of the state system. They do not, of themselves, prove the freedom of religion (a mistake made all too frequently by foreign visitors); they are, in part, a reflection of the serious shortage of functioning churches just about everywhere.

Siberia is much more deprived than European Russia. For example, the major and historic diocese of Irkutsk, the most easterly in the Soviet Union and one of the largest in surface area belonging to any church in the world (no less than 7½ million square kilometres) has a mere 29 churches open, three of which acquired registration in the mid-1970s. This gives an average of less than one church for every quarter of a million square miles. If churches and believers were evenly spaced, the average distance to a church would be over 300 miles. If believers were able to exercise their legal rights, the number of churches or prayer houses in the towns and small settlements would run into hundreds, if not thousands, even in such a sparsely populated area.

Yet, curiously, this very deprivation brings with it some advantages. Having no church in their local community does not prevent Orthodox believers from worshipping, even though they cannot do so every Sunday. Using ingenuity and determination, they will commandeer lorries, even sometimes fly by aeroplane, to reach an open church. Often, even where there are major population centres, the places of worship are located far out in the suburbs or even right in the country. So are the residences of some of the clergy from whom people most want to gather spiritual sustenance. In several Communist countries the clergy who have most pastoral and organisational ability are precisely those who are restricted to country areas where there are few people. But people make considerable efforts to go and consult with them, too, often at certain set times when it is known they hold open house.

The train or bus or hired lorry thus often sees the beginning of a spiritual fellowship among the pilgrims, which flowers and becomes richer the longer the journey is, and often matures over successive journeys, when old friends meet up again. Attempting to impede believers, the Soviet authorities are in fact causing them to recreate something of the spirit of pilgrimage in the medieval world at its best and most spiritual.

The liturgy is therefore journey's end, a moment of great fulfilment. Physical participation—voice, soul and body—marks the liturgy as a congregational experience rarely encountered elsewhere (though less sophisticated societies, such as those in Africa, often come closer to it than their European counterparts).

There are two further factors which enrich the spiritual quality that both clergy and laity pour into the liturgy. Life in the Soviet countryside has very little colour. The drabness of Soviet consumer goods, including clothing, and the uniformity of institutions, all tend to make the liturgy stand out as something attractive and dramatic in a way it does not elsewhere. Then the ban on general parish activities—Bible studies, prayer meetings, social functions and outings—directs the undivided concentration of the whole congregation to this one permitted act, the service of worship. Again, in a curious way, the very restrictions tend to produce an effect which is the precise opposite of that intended by the Soviet authorities. The absence of pews in the Orthodox tradition removes spiritual as well as wooden barriers between people.

The typical church in a major centre of population has two liturgies every day throughout the week, the first at 7am, the second at 9am.[2] There are side chapels which see a succession of rites for individual families, baptisms, funerals and perhaps private counselling. Some churches have several priests who will be kept exhaustingly busy most of the day. The culmination of this long day is vespers at 6pm, with the Saturday evening drawing almost as many as Sunday morning. On Mondays, unless it is a day of special observance, the church is closed. Even though attendance at these services would cut across working hours for the majority of the population, considerably more than a handful of people are there for all the services, naturally predominantly the old at those times.

On Sundays the main liturgy is an hour later, at 10am, and the celebrant is always the parish priest, or the bishop, if it is a cathedral. There are sermons only on Sundays and major festivals, but preaching has become an ever more prominent feature of Orthodox worship in recent years. Homiletics is a major subject on the curriculum of the three theological seminaries, and people seem oblivious of the physical discomfort of standing while listening. Their bodily response to the liturgy, with frequent prostrations and extravagant signs of the cross, is often restricted because of the tight squeeze on Sundays and festivals, though it never loses its spontaneity nor does the desire of worshippers diminish to find their own individual rhythm for these responses.

At the major festivals, notably Easter, only early arrivals have any hope of finding space inside the church building. Those thousands who have to take up positions outside cannot usually follow anything of what is going on inside, because of the restrictions on loud-speaker transmission. They try, in an orderly way, to gain admission at some point, so that they can receive a blessing from the celebrant.

Lest it should be thought that the Soviet set-up provides a model for Christian communities everywhere, it is only fair to note that there are also negative aspects to the controls. The presence of KGB agents at worship is so frequent that worshippers tend to regard themselves as under constant observation. For the majority, the old and those who have no ambition to climb higher on the ladder of promotion at work, there is no cause for worry. For the young or for people doing a job which carries responsibility, the element of intimidation must always be present. As Jane Ellis says, this is 'a barrier to true Christian community, since it renders believers reluctant to talk freely to one another and obviously inhibits their approach to strangers whom they would otherwise wish to welcome into the church.'[3] It does, however, seem that other denominations are less constrained by these controls. Fr Gleb Yakunin, who wrote a major report on the life of the Russian Orthodox Church shortly before his imprisonment in 1979, attributes this to a weak leadership, which could do more to encourage elementary Christian teaching on such obligations. Young people, especially, who have been converted to Orthodoxy, naturally look to it to provide all that has been lacking in their lives heretofore. They are, in many instances, prepared to sacrifice their careers in order to become a regular part of the worshipping community and therefore they take it especially hard when they come face to face with further restrictions upon the religious community itself. A young convert, Alexander Ogorodnikov, writing in 1976, and who was later to suffer long years of imprisonment for activities resulting from his conversion, put it like this:

In the Russian Church the parish is not like a brotherly community where Christian love for one's neighbour becomes a reality. The state persecutes every manifestation of church life, except for the performance of a 'religious cult'. Our thirst for spiritual communion, religious education and missionary service runs up against all the might of the state's repressive machinery.[4]

Hidden Depths

There is much in the life of Russian Orthodoxy that the outside observer, however sympathetic, will never see. Traditional Russian piety has scarcely been touched, let alone controlled or eliminated, by Communism. Naturally this contains elements of popular superstition and would doubtless continue to do so even if religious education and Christian books were properly available, but at the same time it contains a solid stratum of folk wisdom, good sense, neighbourly kindness and personal morality. The Communist ideals which have—unsuccessfully—tried to replace this contain none of these. Orthodoxy remains, in the Russian areas of the Soviet Union, part of the fabric of life, a constituent of the air which people breathe. It is not necessary to ask whether this is part of a 'growing' church: it is, in a miraculous way, a protective cleft in the rock of ages, a demonstration, 70 years after the arrival in power of the world's first atheist regime, that God's power is effortlessly superior to the most elaborate and controlled systems devised by man alone. The Orthodox believer, going to visit his *starets*, his spiritual father, whether priest of a busy parish or holy man living a semi-secret existence in the depth of the Siberian countryside, still comes away from that spiritual communion better equipped to deal with life than many who have received high-powered technical and ideological education from a Soviet university. Sometimes even that very graduate, only too conscious of his spiritual shortcomings, finds his way along the same path.

The power of the Christian faith, not least of Russian Orthodoxy, is quietly pervasive in Siberia, despite the continuing paganism in some areas of the countryside. In the cities it can sometimes come out in to the open and strike any sensitive visitor to the Soviet Far East. One of the present authors has written his impressions of this, following a visit to Irkutsk in 1979.

[Our tourist guide] pre-arranged with the priest of the church in the little village of Listvyanka on the shore of Lake Baikal that he would be there to open the church of St Nicholas for us and to welcome us.

Fr Andronik greeted us warmly at the door of his church under a cloudless sky, with the village behind him sparkling in the piercing clarity of the atmosphere—such a contrast to the industrial pollution of Irkutsk, 50 miles away. Our guide invited us to put questions to him and called me forward to interpret. Fr Andronik is only 29, recently ordained as a monk after starting a career in engineering, which he eventually combined with studying for a theological degree by correspondence course.

He did not say so, but was enthusiastic about his priesthood to date, which had taken him first of all to the one Orthodox church in Ulan-Ude, the capital of the Buryat-Mongol Autonomous Republic, where he had worked 'as though a missionary' among the Buddhists in their main stronghold in the Soviet Union.

I could scarcely believe my ears: I was hearing all this in an 'Intourist' [state-controlled travel agency] context from a young monk, when the official line for decades had been that religion was dying out and no longer played any role worth mentioning in the country at large.

The other official visit was to the Znamensky ('Sign') Convent, which has long since lost its nuns but which has now become the cathedral, replacing the beautiful one right in the city centre a mile away.... But the Znamensky Convent was a hive of activity even in the middle of the afternoon on a working day, two hours before the daily service began.

There must have been 50 old women there, busily engaged in buying candles, praying and crossing themselves. This was nothing compared with the half-full church for the daily liturgy two days later on a Friday morning at eight, when there must have been at least 15 schoolchildren present, not a single one of whom looked as if he had come for any other reason than to pray.[5]

A Man of Service
In Siberia there are many faithful priests serving in conditions similar to those of Fr Andronik or the staff of Irkutsk Cathedral. Under the Soviet system, though the anti-religious zeal or otherwise of the local authorities can modify this generalisation, the more loyal a priest or pastor is to his Christian calling, the more he is likely to fall foul of the law. The popular view, propagated all too often by Christian visitors to the Soviet Union to whom 'disinformation' is passed, is that 'only dissidents and lawbreakers are persecuted'.

Fr Alexander Pivovarov, known among Christians in his locality as the 'light of Siberia', church builder extraordinary, was never a 'dissident' in the conventional sense and would doubtless—and rightly—have disclaimed a role in any movement. His cause was to preach the Christian Gospel and to create in central Siberia better conditions in which this could be done. For many years he proved how much was possible, while working within the system, and the respect and recognition accorded him by his own church leadership is reflected by his appointment as secretary to the Archbishop of Novosibirsk, the reports on his activities published in the *Journal of the Moscow Patriarchate*, and even the articles he wrote for this under his own name. All this was crowded into the early part of his ministry, for he was only 43 when he was arrested in April 1983.

Alexander Pivovarov is a Siberian born at Piisk in the Altai region on 8th July 1939. His parents were believers who endued both him and his sister with a deep love of Christ from their earliest childhood. But they were also young people with enquiring minds, who read widely and quickly learned much about the realities of the world they lived in. His sister became a 'nun in the world', a person who took vows and lived by monastic rules, despite the impossibility of entering a convent.

There being no seminary in Siberia, Alexander entered full-time religious training at Odessa. Though still very young for this, Bishop Pavel of Novosibirsk, himself well known as one of the most independent spirits in the Orthodox Church, ordained him at the age of 21, just after his marriage (essential in the Orthodox tradition for non-monastic priests) to a young woman who proved an admirable companion in his life's work. He went on to a higher degree at the theological academy at Zagorsk. Turning down an offer to work in the External Relations Department of the Moscow Patriarchate (with its attendant attractions of foreign travel), he went back to Siberia to begin the parochial ministry which he had always felt was his true calling.

Even at this stage, his powerful preaching and personal faith attracted the attention of the authorities, slanderous articles appeared about him in the local press, but he had broken no law, and, in the slightly easier conditions which prevailed following the fall of Khrushchev in 1964, they left him alone.

To carry out even minor maintenance work on the fabric of church buildings is often impossible, yet everywhere he served he left behind him a legacy in bricks and mortar, as well as in the conversion of souls. The *Journal of the Mos-*

cow Patriarchate reported the remarkable and rare fact that he had built a new church at Novokuznetsk. Situated in the coal and iron-ore region of the Kuzbass, this city saw massive industrial expansion in the 1930s to the extent that it became regarded as a kind of model Soviet city—and certainly one from which God would be visibly absent—and even received the accolade of having its name changed to 'Stalinsk', though of course later it was embarrassingly necessary to revert to the old name. Later he extended the churches at Tomsk and Prokopevsk by building new baptismal chapels with altars.

For a decade petty harassment was never far away, though his immense theological learning, allied to his spiritual authority and his practical good sense, acted as a kind of shield against the ignorance and petty-mindedness of the local authorities. His appointment in 1975 as secretary to Gedeon, the new Archbishop of Novosibirsk, was not only recognition of his major contribution, but also in a very real sense an act of protection. Wherever he was, his church had always been one to which people constantly made pilgrimages such as we described above. It was always a beacon of light to Christians for perhaps thousands of miles around. Now, in the major centre of Novosibirsk he was accessible literally to millions and his influence began to spread as widely as was physically possible under Soviet conditions.

In the *Journal of the Moscow Patriarchate* we read that this influence was international. Foreign guests came, and he was in charge of their programme. Its pages bear testimony of people from as far afield as Yugoslavia and the United States listening to his sermons.[6] There is no doubt, and the *Journal* produces the evidence, that he was involved in the building of further churches in the diocese during this time.

But for Fr Alexander Pivovarov church buildings were only the shell. Spiritual instruction was the substance and in this Christian literature, virtually non-existent under Soviet conditions, must play a role. Perhaps the most impressive testimony to his impact on non-believers (as well as on the faithful themselves) comes from an atheist source. The 'Furov Report' is a leaked secret document prepared for the Council on Religious Affairs in 1975. Its main purpose was to assess the 'reliability', from the point of view of Soviet atheism, of various leading clergy. It singled out Fr Alexander as one of the most outstanding evangelists of the Russian Orthodox Church, a man of colossal energy and organisation who was a perpetual missionary in his own far-flung diocese—and this refers to a time while he was still officially bound to one parish, just before he became secretary to the Archbishop of Novosibirsk.

On the initiative of the priest 'A I Pivovarov', the report tells us, the clergy of the region increased their influence. In 1974, at the beginning of Lent, he took the lead in announcing from the pulpit that believers from any town or village could invite a priest to their houses, which was followed by a flood of invitations to the clergy from all and sundry. They exploited the law permitting services at home for the seriously ill to involve people who were, to all intents and purposes, healthy. Clergy descended upon the countryside and he himself visited at least four different districts, preceded by an emissary who 'announced his arrival and prepared a place for the service, after which the priest arrived to carry out collective rites.'[7] Two men accompanied him who allegedly organised the sale of religious objects.

Each of the priests' journeys to a district where he had not been for several years incited the religious feelings of believers, gave rise to an unhealthy interest among unbelievers and those indifferent to religion, and served the cause of religious propaganda.[8]

The passage concluded with an ominous phrase to the effect that 'measures have been taken' to terminate such visitations. Whatever the measures, the church's countermeasure was to promote Fr Alexander to a position where

His trial in Novosibirsk followed in August, lasting nine days.

As with the Moscow group, the rigging of the evidence made it appear that Fr Alexander was accused of buying and selling for profit. Only the sketchiest account of the trial has become available. When he entered the courtroom on the first day, he discovered that a number of his parishioners, friends and relatives had been able to gain access to it. He greeted them with the proclamation of the Resurrection, the universal Easter greeting of the Orthodox Church—'Christ is risen'—to which the response came from within the courtroom, 'He is risen indeed.'

The details of what happened during the subsequent days are virtually lacking and concerned only with a few instances of who sold what book or cross to whom and at what price. As the defence lawyer submitted, it was clear that even under Soviet law no crime had been committed, but the verdict was guilty: four years' imprisonment and confiscation of property. On hearing this, Fr Alexander looked around the courtroom, fell on his knees and pronounced his blessing upon everyone present, believer and non-believer alike.

A later report states that the sentence was commuted and he was given a conditional discharge. It is not known whether he has been able to resume his pastoral ministry.

After 1,000 years of existence in Russia, the Orthodox Church has a perspective on a different plane from Communism. Far from needing to make concessions in order to guarantee the future, its very timelessness, coupled with the dedication of young priests like Fr Alexander Pivovarov, gives it prospects of extraordinary promise for the future.

Chapter 10

Moscow Orthodox: Revival in the Heartland

Russian Christians have their treasure in earthen vessels just like anyone else. They are not supermen existing on a different plane. They can be tempted and fall or draw back just when facing a crucial hurdle. Undeniably, among them are men and women of amazing heroism, but when one takes in a perspective of the whole vast land, one notes that these are individuals, perhaps an army, but not a whole church.

From time to time the Holy Spirit uses one person for a task of special responsibility, animating him in a unique way to go beyond his physical or mental powers in the service of the kingdom. The outstanding ministry of Fr Dimitri Dudko had an outcome which many people have considered tragic, even a betrayal. Yet this intimidated, apparently broken man, serving at Peski, about 60 miles south east of Moscow, is still a force for good in the spiritual revival which gathers strength within the Russian Orthodox Church. To play such a role, you do not have to be an activist in the human rights movement, just as Fr Alexander Pivovarov was not. In the very final analysis, the Christian future of the Soviet Union does depend, if one had to choose, more on spiritual subjugation to the commands of Christ than on high-profile campaigning for religious liberty, however necessary both unquestionably are.

The most active Russian Orthodox priests are forced to be unnaturally mobile. As soon as they build up a sizable local following, the authorities press for their removal to a new place. Therefore, to make the concept of 'growing' churches meaningful in the Soviet context, it is sometimes necessary to see the growth in terms of the spiritual influence radiating from one individual, wherever he may be.

A Preacher Extraordinary

As a young man in the immediate post-war period, Fr Dimitri spent no less than eight-and-a-half years in a labour camp, years followed eventually by an amnesty. Although this seriously interrupted his theological education and postponed his ordination until 1960, the experience nevertheless was the psychological foundation of his life, showing him the full range of fallen humanity, deepening his own spiritual resources and identifying him with the lot of so many others who had suffered under Stalin. In devastating the flower of his youth, it also showed him the lengths to which the Soviet system could go in meting out injustice, making the fear of a repetition ever present in his mind. By 1962, at the age of 40, he had settled into the parish of St Nicholas in the Transfiguration Cemetery in Moscow, which became the focal point for the best-known part of his ministry.

It is not often that one thinks of the sheer physical demands, not to mention spiritual, in running a Moscow parish. If each of the 43 churches is staffed by three priests, on the average, there are still fewer than 150 priests engaged in pastoral work in a city of nearly 9 million people. (It is not yet known how many new priests will reside in the recently-opened Danilovsky Monastery). To state that this is one priest for every 210,000 of population is totally misleading because of the flood of visitors, not only from the surrounding countryside, but also from the furthest corners of the Soviet Union, many of whom are denied any regular Christian ministration where they live.

For many priests adult baptisms alone average 10–12 a week, with every individual needing personal instruction beforehand. Fr Dimitri said that beyond this the number of children was countless. Then there are weddings, some ministry to the housebound at home, and funerals. It is not clear how time is ever found at all for preparation for preaching, let alone the spiritual reflection that should precede and accompany celebration of the liturgy. It is doubtful whether Christian ministry worldwide offers many more daunting tasks. How can the KGB find a slot for the interrogations that must inevitably follow when the work of a priest seems to them too successful?

Fr Dimitri kept up this pace for two decades, except that for him in the middle of that time it increased considerably. Alexander Solzhenitsyn and his wife, Natalya, frequently visited his church from about 1969. Natalya well represents the man and the demands of the ministry at this period:

The return to the church in those years was not yet a mass one, as it is now, but it was already having a noticeable influence on the general atmosphere of society. People were seeking living words about God, seeking spiritual preceptors. It was not easy to find them…. There were not good pastors in every church. But all the same, people found Fr Dimitri and came to him endlessly. With him you could meet young women with children, elderly men, youths, well-known writers, artists and perfectly ordinary residents of the surrounding villages…. Very Russian in spirit, he is also very Russian in appearance: thickset with a large head and bright blue eyes. He is affectionately attentive to everybody, he listens and does not say much about himself, but after every encounter with him you are left with the feeling: how deep and joyful is his faith! He is a man of surprising integrity and simplicity, and his preaching finds a direct and accurate path to a person's heart.[1]

As early as 1972 the eye of the KGB had alighted on Fr

Dimitri's popularity and the question of his dismissal inevitably arose. His preaching, as Mrs Solzhenitsyn indicated, was already a notable feature of his ministry, so he chose to 'cross the line' for the first time. This line, undrawn in geometrical or legal terms, nevertheless exists; pastors know fairly clearly where it is (though its position is modified by local conditions and Communist attitudes) and cross it at their peril. No law censors sermons. Yet everyone knows that a whole range of subjects is taboo. You do not encourage prayer for prisoners or build up a delineated counter-offensive against atheism, for example, without crossing that line. Fr Dimitri went decisively over it when he appealed to the congregation to support him in his struggle to remain as their pastor. In one passage he reflected on the horrors of the 'Great Patriotic War' (as World War II is called in the Soviet Union)—no danger in exploiting another vein leading off that overworked seam. But he then crossed the line again by referring to present moral dangers every bit as threatening as the physical ones of 30 years earlier. Vice was 'corrupting families and morally crippling the rising generation', with a notable increase in 'drunkness, hooliganism and murder.'[2]

Although the Soviet press is allowed to mention social evils such as drunkenness, the propaganda view is that the overall moral standards in society have risen beyond recognition since the advent of Communism. Christian tradition would enable the church to collaborate with the state in its efforts to bring about a real improvement, but it receives an instantaneous rebuttal if it tries (which does not, of course, prevent it from doing so behind the scenes).

The sermon went on to mention his own imprisonment as an example of the lawlessness of the past and then he referred to the monitoring of his congregation's activities, which was quite illegal under laws which proclaimed the separation of church and state. The very naturalness with which he introduced taboo subjects which were, nevertheless, well known to his listeners, deeply impressed itself upon all who heard him and prepared the way for the next stage in his ministry. For the time being, the authorities took no further direct action against him.

Perhaps too much emphasis in the West has been placed on the 'conversations', or question-and-answer sessions which Fr Dimitri Dudko inaugurated after his Saturday evening services the next year. We must never forget that they were, however unprecedented in Soviet conditions and on the wrong side of the line, a very simple form of teaching ministry and no more than an adjunct to the demanding pastoral work which we have outlined above. In any democratic country this 'normal' development would not have aroused the slightest interest outside the congregation itself. It was the KGB, of course, which magnified what happened into a highly-contentious issue.

Fr Dimitri announced his intention as an initiative in Christian education and it is clear, both from his intention and from an analysis of the texts of the 'conversations' which we have, that this was not an entry into the human-rights debate, even less a challenge to Soviet legislation.[3] People would be helped to understand the Orthodox liturgy, guided in prayer and Bible study.

In order to ensure decorum, written questions were to be handed in anonymously if desired. Fr Dimitri would select questions, group them together in themes and answer later. So immediately did these talks respond to the spiritual needs of the Russian people that within a week or two after they began in December 1973 people were flocking from far afield to hear them.

A Russian observer who was present (Anatoli Levitin, now resident in Switzerland) recorded that they made an impact on many intellectuals who had had no previous contact with the Christian faith. It was the young especially who came, and a Baptist would find himself rubbing shoulders with a Zen Buddhist. All were equally impressed by his 'sincerity, simplicity and enormous conviction; chiefly by his sincerity.'[4] He could, in the simplest language, elicit a personal response from those present, just as if he was addressing everyone present individually and alone. Even reading out passages from Christian books was valuable, because these were not available to people in any bookshop or library.

Even in such a short series, which continued only until May 1974, certain recurring themes emerged. He constantly returned to the basic contradiction at the heart of the Christian faith: suffering leads to resurrection. Assuredly, he maintained, this very same drama was being enacted in the Soviet Union today. From this he would move on to delineate the conflict that there must inevitably be with atheism, which had brought so many negative consequences into Russian life:

By undermining faith in God, atheism has also undermined all bases of social life ... immorality, the collapse of the family, criminality and hooliganism—these are the fruits of atheism.... I don't think this will go on much longer.... There are believers everywhere—among scholars, as well as the simple.... I'm sure I've baptised at least 5,000 adults.[5]

Not only the Soviet press but also the pronouncements of Soviet church leaders at conferences abroad constantly hammer home the message that Soviet society has eliminated class hatred and therefore the bases of injustice. When his congregation heard Fr Dimitri saying the opposite, they instantaneously knew that he was right, and they responded in their hearts. Crossing the line and yet doing it in such a spiritual way strengthened the faith of believers, but it also set many hundreds of unbelievers on their first decisive step towards faith.

So impressive were his words that he could touch the heart even of a 'capitalist' atheist, a young Englishman, who summed up his experience in these words:

What did it all mean? Well, to me, then an atheist, just this. The immorality of Soviet society—its inhumanity and corruption, its lack of a moral code or credible ideals—means that Christ's teaching comes through to those whom it reaches as a shining contrast. It stresses the value of the individual, of humaneness, forgiveness, gentleness, love.... As for me, the atheist, Fr Dimitri that evening convinced me that the moral code of Christianity was not just something that could be cast aside as superseded; that, in fact, it had survived for 2,000 years precisely because it did stress certain qualities essential in personal relations between men. The loss of these qualities is one of the most disturbing features of modern Soviet life.[6]

At this point an unsettling element enters into the story. There are many previous examples where the KGB has leaned upon the church hierarchy to carry out the act of suppression. Whereas the Bishop of Novosibirsk clearly protected Fr Alexander Pivovarov in 1975 by appointing him as his own secretary, as we saw in the previous chapter, the Moscow Patriarchate on its home ground, but undoubtedly also under a much more watchful political eye, could do no more than transfer him to a parish outside the city, thereby breaking up his following and reducing his profile.

On 4th May Fr Dimitri announced that there would be no talk, because the Patriarch had forbidden it. Two weeks later he stated in church that his attempts to have a personal meeting with the head of the Church had come to nothing, but instead the Patriarch's secretary had demanded a written explanation of all that had been going on. This he supplied, but it made no difference to the decision to transfer him. He left the church in the company of two young men, who turned out to be believers protecting their priest, not the KGB arresting him, as many thought when they saw him being taken to a waiting car.

On 20th May Metropolitan Serafim of Krutitsy, the senior cleric responsible for the Moscow diocese, banned him from priestly office for 'ignoring church discipline', until such time as he should repent.

Thus far the response of the authorities in hiding behind the church leadership and the pressure brought were entirely predictable and had happened in previous instances. What was not predictable was Fr Dimitri's rapid compliance with the instruction to repent, even though extreme humility towards high ecclesiastical authority is a trait ingrained in the Orthodox tradition. There was also, it seems likely, some inclination to self-abasement in his own character, which was to lead him into such personal tragedy later. He wrote to Metropolitan Serafim that any infraction of church discipline had been involuntary, but he was now ready to appear before the Metropolitan, as opposed to insisting on an audience with the Patriarch, and to accept whatever judgement there should be.

The meeting took place. The ensuing transfer to the village of Kabanovo 50 miles from Moscow was a relatively mild 'punishment' for an influential pastor, but at the same time illustrated starkly just how direct could be the interference of the secular authorities in the affairs of a registered church in a country where the constitution proclaims separation of church and state. But from the point of view of the proclamation of the Kingdom of God, the next stage in Fr Dimitri Dudko's ministry illustrates very clearly the concept of the 'mobile parish'. Obviously, the good people of Kabanovo benefitted immensely from the presence of an outstanding pastor among them (even though his actual residence was still the same Moscow flat) and perhaps in a much smaller community than the anonymity of Moscow the ministry of one man was more clearly identifiable. But for the converts, especially the young and energetic, that ministry remained essentially unchanged, or perhaps even more focussed.

They came to him as they had done before, but now they would assemble on one platform of one railway station and climb aboard one train, ardently discussing among themselves the moral and social issues with which the challenge of the Gospel was presenting them. Visiting Fr Dimitri's church in Kabanovo was now already a pilgrimage, a spiritual and physical exercise imposed upon the faithful by the Soviet authorities, but leading directly to the weaving of a much more closely-knit community. We can never know of more than a tiny proportion of the offshoots of this ministry or the names of more than a few individuals here and there affected by it, but when one notes that Alexander Ogorodnikov, who was to go on to found the remarkable 'Christian Seminar',[7] considered Fr Dimitri to be his 'spiritual father' (as the Orthodox describe those under whose instruction they come), it is immediately obvious that we are talking about a major and enduring example of Christian growth, the secret facets of which will eventually come into the full light of day.

Mounting Threats

If one of the motives of the church authorities in transferring Fr Dimitri to Kabanovo was to afford him a measure of protection, this failed. There was no respite from the rumbling background of half-veiled threats from the authorities. It seemed that his continuing preaching and pastoral work drew on resources which were far deeper than the man himself.

Even at the time of the Moscow 'conversations' he had seemed to some a frail figure to be standing against the fury of the Soviet atheists. One observer could not understand how he could continue, because he seemed to be cast in so much more timid a mould than Solzhenitsyn, who was 'afraid of nothing and nobody, but this man is afraid all the time—yet he carries on.'[8]

After no more than six months at Kabanovo his ministry there was cut short by a very serious car accident, which was certainly an attempt on his life. In March 1975 he was a passenger in a car, when a lorry reversed without warning into his side of the vehicle and drove away in haste without stopping. Further, the militia obstructed any subsequent attempt to trace the driver or to investigate the circumstances. Even though his life was saved (one source said a great Bible he had been holding protected his chest), both legs were broken and he had to face a long convalescence, which of course prevented him from celebrating the liturgy, or even from having pastoral contact with the people of Kabanovo, as he did not live there and for a long time could not travel.

He had still not made a complete recovery when, at the end of the year, he was dismissed from the parish, after being there only 15 months, for over half of which time he had been a cripple. Over 300 of his parishioners, people who had never been involved in human rights activities, signed an appeal against his dismissal to the Soviet authorities, and in it they underlined especially the value of his sermons, which had been instrumental in creating a 'healthy spiritual atmosphere in our church'.[9]

On 13th January 1976 Metropolitan Serafim went way beyond his previous criticism of a priest under his personal direction and claimed, in a sentence which sounds as if it had been written by an atheist rather than a church leader, that the parish executive committee had cancelled their priest's contract because 'he had systematically included in his sermons and talks political material of an anti-social character, containing tendentious criticism of the life of our state'.[10] There was further criticism of him for having used a small parish house to receive people who came out from Moscow to hear his sermons.

Before long he was transferred to Grebnevo, a village situated a similar two-hour train journey away from the capital, this time to the south-east. It is hard to see how anyone expected this to change the basic nature of Fr Dimitri's ministry.

In June 1976 he was one of 27 signatories of a remarkable ecumenical appeal, signed by members of six denominations and aimed, in part, at bringing the World Council of Churches much more closely into touch with what was really happening in the Soviet Union on the religious front. A much more controversial activity was to join in a campaign for the canonisation of martyrs of the Soviet period, including the last Tsar, Nicholas II, who had been murdered by the Bolsheviks. This lost him some support among his friends, both at home and abroad, but in any normal society could have occasioned a sensible debate, as opposed to being interpreted as a challenge to the regime, which he certainly did not intend.

The campaign of vilification against Fr Dimitri took a much more serious turn when on 13th and 20th April 1977 one of the most influential Soviet newspapers, the *Literary Gazette*, published a scurrilous attack against him and three others, heralding the most serious crackdown against the Orthodox Church for 12 years.

Quite unfairly, this attack characterised the group as passing false information on religious persecution to the West, a practice which gave enemies of the Soviet Union the opportunity to vilify the system. Beyond this, Fr Dimitri's individual 'crime' was influencing young people towards the faith who happened casually to 'glance into' his church.

It is true that his mobile ministry, in transferring to Grebnevo, was continuing as before. It is equally true that his ministry to young people (which did not include systematic instruction classes for young people under the age of 18) broke no Soviet law. There was specific criticism of his evil influence on one girl in particular, but she, with outstanding bravery, responded by writing a resounding defence of her pastor to the editor of the newspaper. She said that he had given her sound advice during a period of family tension and disunity. Far from being the bewildered and duped victim represented in the article, she said that as an independent and adult person, she found it 'impossible to write about Dimitri Sergeyevich [Dudko] without acknowledging my debt of gratitude to him'. In the pastor's spiritual parish there would have been many hundreds to echo that sentiment, even if they were not all brave enough to express it so openly. This must have more than made up for the infiltration by the KGB of the ranks of his 'spiritual children', some of whom abandoned him and caused trouble. Others were put under considerable pressure, but stood firm. During one raid on the parish room on 11th September 1978 Vladimir Sedov was thrown out into the snow and severely beaten. Despite this, young people kept coming in large crowds to hear the preaching and to receive counsel. The KGB even threatened the priest's own son with psychiatric detention.

The evidence of Alexander Ogorodnikov illustrates how one seed sown can bear most remarkable fruit. This young man became a convert to the Christian faith from an atheist background while a student at the Institute of Cinematography in Moscow and the influence of Fr Dimitri was one of the factors which helped his growth and development as a Christian. Ogorodnikov, in his turn, had a major influence on dozens of young people by establishing the 'Christian Seminar', which itself was later disbanded after a series of swoops by the KGB resulting in the arrest of all the leading figures.

Far from being intimidated into non-activity by the endless harassment, although physically exhausted, Fr Dimitri crossed the invisible line once again. In September 1978 he established a parish magazine, something unknown in the Soviet Union. *In the Light of the Transfiguration* did for one locality what Soviet Baptists had been trying for over a decade to do for the whole country: to report news of parishioners, including any illegality or discrimination to which they had been subjected, and to print devotional articles and spiritual advice, including answers to questions the faithful themselves had raised.

No Christian activity could have been more normal. Yet under Soviet conditions even such a modest adjunct to the building up of the spiritual life of his growing church came into the category of illegal activities to be suppressed. The net was closing round him, and it could not be held back by the group of faithful, young and old, who surrounded him and his family with love and care. For three years in Grebnevo the spiritual work went on amid unending threats and difficulties, not least the pain caused by the arrest and savage sentences passed on other outstanding figures in the Russian Orthodox Church and on some of his own spiritual children. Sadly absent was any sign of support from the Moscow Patriarchate.

Arrest

The arrest of Fr Dimitri finally came early in the morning of 15th January 1980. The illegality of it is underlined by the accompanying house search and confiscation of masses of material which could have no conceivable criminal significance, such as Christian literature, his typewriter and personal money. Not only had he not committed any crime: he had specifically not been part of the growing human rights movement within the Orthodox Church and was the registered pastor of a registered parish, which two factors were supposed—in Soviet propaganda—to be a guarantee against action by the state.

There was a flood of protest, both in East and West, when the maw of the Lefortovo jail engulfed Fr Dimitri. Even a white South African Anglican priest under a banning order wrote in protest, while a senior official of the Patriarchate described Fr Dimitri as a 'nervous and unbalanced person' who would be liable to break the law.[11]

Such undermining of Fr Dimitri's moral position must be one factor in the tragedy which ensued, but it is not the major one. We may never know the psychological and possibly physical torture by administration of drugs which, over the next five months, led Fr Dimitri to betray much of what he had stood for and to admit to crimes he had never committed.

Church and state vied with each other to publish his admission of criminal guilt. Television, the Soviet press and the *Journal of the Moscow Patriarchate* carried his confession to pride, 'anti-Soviet slander' and the supply of information for the West to discredit his country. He renounced his 'so-called struggle with godlessness as a struggle with Soviet power'. He listed some of his supposedly illegitimate contacts with foreigners and ended by begging the Patriarch to receive him back into his flock 'as a newborn child'.[12] His later letter to the patriarchate was even more self-abasing.

It takes no profound observation to see that the real tragedy here was within the church leadership itself, seen here colluding with the atheist authorities in suppressing the work of a great evangelist to which there had been unprecedented response among the people. Since 1927, when Metropolitan Sergius was forced into swearing loyalty to the atheist tyranny of Stalin's Russia, there had not been many quite such open examples of the church leadership's being forced to work against the interests of the Kingdom of God. In the sorry episode it was the Moscow Patriarchate rather than Fr Dimitri Dudko who suffered the true humiliation. For the priest, the story of those hidden five months explains all, even without our knowing any of the details. Even the 'mistake' we know he made of trying to convert his interrogator, Vladimir Sorokin, was not a mistake in the eyes of God.

We may spend time analysing Fr Dimitri's state of mind both before and after the imprisonment, as Jane Ellis does dispassionately in her book; we may speculate on inborn weaknesses in his character which predisposed him to confess when the pressure was on; we may discuss the effect which his recantation had upon his hundreds of spiritual children and upon his thousands of supporters in the West. None of this even begins to challenge the right of Fr Dimitri and his ministry to occupy a key place among the 'growing churches' of the Soviet Union.

Fr Dimitri has nurtured tens of thousands of ordinary people by exercising a faithful and regular pastoral ministry in registered churches over three decades, showing them that the traditional Orthodox Church watches over and cares for them. To hundreds of young people, many from atheist backgrounds, he has presented the faith as not only something which lives, but which challenges their perception of society and the world and which is relevant to the future of a country which officially renounced God 70 years ago. Many of those seeds sown have germinated, grown into plants and now flower in unknown places, some already scattering their own crop of new seeds.

Meanwhile Fr Dimitri, always a frightened man, who yet overcame his fear over many years, underwent more suffering as a result of his renunciation than he did while in Lefortovo prison. As he fought with himself to express the bitterness of his remorse for his betrayal, it seemed that the effects of whatever they did to him were wearing off, and yet at the same time renewed threats intimidated him once again. He indicated surprise that not even his friends in the West could read between the lines of his confession—if he renounced 'illegal' contacts with the West, could people not see that he was in fact holding fast to them, for they broke no Soviet law? In one of the newsletters which he continued to write, he stated, 'I voluntarily took the path of shame, in order to do something further'.[13] This identified him even more deeply with one of the mainstreams of Russian spirituality, a tendency to self-abasement before God.

That 'something further' continues even now. Vinogradovo, Voskresensk, and now Peski—all within 100 miles south-east of Moscow and fairly easily accessible—the faithful in all these places have successively benefitted from his ministry. Someone who has known the utter loneliness of Gethsemane and who has, at least mentally, experienced the unjust suffering of the Cross, still has something to offer to those in trouble and need. Who is to judge that the lower profile of Fr Dimitri's ministry since 1980 is worth one whit the less in the sight of God than what he was doing so dramatically before his last imprisonment?

Writing of Fr Dimitri's tragedy, one of his spiritual children reveals the tension between the persecution and the
growth of Soviet Christianity today. His words are a fitting
epilogue to the whole book.

We know all too well what measures can be employed in such
cases. This could have happened to any one of us ... we can never
forget that Fr Dimitri has brought the light of God to thousands of
people. Now the authorities want to make him pay by discrediting
him ... by sowing the seeds of doubt among the faithful about his
spiritual integrity. However, what Fr Dimitri has accomplished
over the past 20 years cannot be wiped out.[14]

FOOTNOTES

Chapter 1

1 As in Finland, the Orthodox Church in Estonia prac-
   tised confirmation, so as to build a comparable youth
   commitment to that in the dominant Lutheran Church.
   On the new Soviet rituals, see Vello Salo, 'Anti-religious Rites in Estonia', *Religion in Communist Lands*
   (henceforth *RCL*), the journal of Keston College, Vol
   I, Nos 4–5, 1973, pp 28–33.

2 *RCL*, Vol I, Nos 4–5, 1973, p 32.

3 *Ibid*.

4 This section draws on Peter Stephens, 'The Methodist
   Church of Eastern Europe', *RCL*, Vol V, No 1, 1977,
   pp. 15–18.

5 *Voprosy nauchnogo ateizma (VNA)* is the journal of the
   Institute of Scientific Atheism, Moscow. 'The Missio-
   nary and Preaching Activity of the Estonian Methodist
   Church', unsigned, is in No 24, 1980, pp 169–80.

6 *Ibid*, pp 172–73.

7 *Now*, Methodist Overseas Division, London, November 1976, p 15.

8 *VNA*, 1979, p 174.

9 *Ibid*.

10 *Ibid*, pp 174–75.

11 *Ibid*, pp 176–77.

12 *Ibid*, pp 178–79.

13 Typewritten document, '*The Methodist Church in Estonia: Superintendent's Circular Letter*', No 76, May 1979, p 1 (in Keston College Archive).

14 *Methodist Recorder*, London, 24th January 1985, p 10.

15 *Ibid*.

16 *Ibid*.

17 *Methodist Recorder*, 15th August 1985, pp 1 and 13.

Chapter 2
1 Harri Mõtsnik, *What is Needed for Peace?* a collection of sermons published in English, with introduction by Archbishop Konrad Veem, Stockholm, 1986, p 57. The translations used here are adapted where necessary.

2 *Ibid*, pp 15–18.

3 *Ibid*, p 6.

4 *Ibid*, p 30.

5 *Ibid* pp 21–22.

6 *Ibid*, p 52.

7 *Ibid*, pp 23–26.

8 *Ibid*, pp 12–14.

9 *Ibid*, pp 46–47.

10 *Ibid*, p 2.

11 *Sovetskaya Estonia*, Tallinn, 19th February 1986, p 3.

Chapter 3
1 Unpublished document in Keston College Archive.

2 *Kommunistichesky trud*, Chuguyevka, 16th July 1985 (reprinted from *Krasnoye znamya*, Vladivostok, 11th July 1985).

3 *Ibid*.

4 See Lorna Bourdeaux, *Valeri Barinov: The Trumpet Call* (Marshalls: Basingstoke, Hants, 1985), p 151.

5 Unpublished document in Keston College Archive.

6 *Ibid*.

7 24th November 1984, presumably in the Chuguyevka local paper, *Kommunistichesky trud*, quoted in document in Keston College Archive.

Chapter 4

1 *Keston News Service* (henceforth *KNS*), fortnightly news bulletin of Keston College, No 245, 6th March 1986, p 17.

2 H and G Woelk, *A Wilderness Journey*, Centre for Mennonite Brethren Studies, Fresno, California, 1982. The quotations are included here by permission of the publishers, who point out that not all Mennonites agree with the standpoint of the authors. We have adapted the translation where necessary.

3 *A Wilderness Journey*, pp 36–37.

4 *Ibid*, pp 38–39.

5 The Woelks are the source of most of the information which follows.

6 *A Wilderness Journey*, p 33.

7 *Ibid*, p 83.

8 *Ibid*, p 86.

9 *Ibid*.

10 *Ibid*, p 90.

11 *Ibid*, p 113.

12 *Ibid*, p 114.

13 *Ibid*, p 156.

14 *Ibid*, p 164.

Chapter 5

1 *Bratsky vestnik*, Moscow, 5, 1982, pp 48–56 and 1, 1983, pp 24–34.

2 Walter Sawatsky, *Soviet Evangelicals since World War II*, Kitchener, Ontario, 1981, p 40.

3 See Michael Bourdeaux, *Religious Ferment in Russia*, London, 1968, and *Faith on Trial in Russia*, London, 1971.

4 L N Mitrokhin, *Baptizm*, Moscow, 1966, pp 74–89.

5 *Evangelical Christians–Baptists in the USSR*, AU-CECB, Moscow, 1971, p 23.

6 See Michael Bourdeaux, *Opium of the People*, London, 1965, p 167, for a comment on the earlier standard.

7 Sawatsky, *op cit*, p 110.

8 Michael Bourdeaux, *Opium of the People*, p 167.

9 See Lorna Bourdeaux, *Barinov: The Trumpet Call*, pp 137–38.

10 *Trud* (Labour), Moscow, 6th July 1984.

11 Mitrokhin, *op cit*, p 163.

12 *Baptizm i gumanizm*, Moscow, 1967, p 76.

13 Yu V Gagarin, *Yevangelskiye Khristianye–Baptisty*, Syktyvkar, 1966, p 57.

Chapter 6
1 See Michael Bourdeaux, *Religious Ferment in Russia*, for a detailed account of the origins and effect of the schism.

2 Walter Sawatsky, *Soviet Evangelicals since World War II*.

3 *Eben-ezer*, unpublished document in Keston College Archive, Kharkov, 1977, pp 3–4.

4 *Ibid*, p 4.

5 *Gospel Call*, Pasadena, California, March 1974, p 5.

6 *Bulletin of the Council of Prisoners' Relatives*, unpublished document in Keston College Archive, No 12, 1973, p 15.

Chapter 7
1 Quoted in *RCL*, Vol 11, No 3, Winter 1983, p 278.

2 *Ibid*, p 283.

3 *Ibid*, pp 283–84.

4 *Ibid*, p 290.

5 *Ibid*, p 291.

6 *Chronicle of the Catholic Church in Ukraine*, No 4, April–May 1984.

7 *RCL*, Vol 11, No 3, p 290.

8 *Ibid*, p 293.

9 *KNS* 240, 12th December 1985, p 15.

10 *Radyans'ka Ukrayina*, Kiev, 28th June 1983.

11 *Chronicle of the Catholic Church in Ukraine*, No 1, January 1984.

12 *Chronicle of the Catholic Church in Ukraine*, No 6, June–July 1984.

13 *Lvovskaya pravda*, Lviv, 3rd April 1985.

14 *RCL*, Vol 11, No 3, p 290.

Chapter 8
1 Michael Bourdeaux, *Land of Crosses*, Chulmleigh, Devon, 1979, p 242.

2 *Ibid*, p 190.

3 *Ibid*, p 185.

4 *Ibid*, p 186.

5 *Ibid*, pp 207–8.

6 *Ibid*, p 211.

7 *Ibid*, p 212.

8 *KNS* 184, 6th October 1983, p 16.

9 *KNS* 192, 9th February 1984, p 7.

10 *KNS* 210, 11th October 1984, pp 8–9.

Chapter 9

1 Croom Helm, Beckenham, 1986.

2 See Jane Ellis, *The Russian Orthodox Church*, pp 39–77, for a fuller account of normal parish life.

3 *Ibid*, p 41.

4 *Ibid*, p 42.

5 Michael Bourdeaux, 'To Siberia—and back', *Church Times*, 4th May 1979, p 11.

6 *Journal of the Moscow Patriarchate*, Moscow, No 4, 1981, p 21.

7 *Furov Report*, p 18. Russian original unpublished. Full text in Keston College Archive.

8 *Ibid*.

Chapter 10

1 Quoted in Jane Ellis, *The Russian Orthodox Church*, p 310. I am indebted to this book for virtually all the information which follows. Because of the demands of construction, Miss Ellis had to spread her telling of Fr Dimitri Dudko's story over several sections of the book. She has generously agreed to my recounting it here.

2 *Ibid*, p 310.

3 *Our Hope*, by Dmitrii Dudko, St Vladimir's Seminary Press, New York, 1977. This book is the text of the 'conversations'.

4 Ellis, *op cit*, p 312.

5 *Ibid*.

6 *Ibid*. pp 312–13.

7 *Ibid*, pp 381–91.

8 *Ibid*, p 315.

9 *Ibid*, p 410.

10 *Ibid*.

11 *Ibid*, p 425.

12 *Ibid*, p 431.

13 *Ibid*, p 436.

14 *Ibid*, p 433.

Appendix 1

Religious Statistics: The Soviet Union

Statistical Case History—The Russian Orthodox Church under Communism

	1914	1939	1947–57	1962	1980
Dioceses	73	?	73	73	73
Bishops in diocesan service	163	c.4	74	63	64
Parish clergy	51,105	100s	c.20,000	14,000	6,000
Churches	54,174	100s	c.18,000	11,500	7,500
Monasteries and convents	1,025	nil	67	32	16–20
Monks and nuns	94,629	?	c.10,000	5,000	?
Church academies	4	nil	2	2	2
Theological seminaries	57	nil	8	5	3
Pre-theological schools	185				
Parochial Schools	37,528		FORBIDDEN BY LAW		
Hospitals	291				
Homes for the aged	1,113				
Parish libraries	34,497				

Buddhists
Old Believers
Adventists, Lutherans, Methodists, Pentecostals, Mennonites
Baptists
Armenian Apostolic
Uniates
Georgian Orthodox
Roman Catholics
Muslims
Russian Orthodox
No religion

Population in millions

0   25   50   75   100   125   150

Accurate statistics on religious affiliation in the Soviet Union are impossible to discover.

Appendix 2

LAWS

The activities of religious believers are subject not only to published laws, but also to secret directives. The Council for Religious Affairs is the government body which supervises religious activities. It communicates these secret laws to its local representatives. Believers are not informed about their content or existence. Some secret laws which believers suspected to exist were introduced into the revised legislation on religion in 1975 and so became public for the first time.

Religious believers are permitted to:
attend services of worship in a church or building which has been registered for that purpose. Church funds can be used only for the maintenance of that building.

Religious groups are forbidden to:
use funds for any kind of charitable or social work;

give material help to their members;

organise meetings for children—Sunday schools, outings or other activities;

form youth clubs or youth groups;

hold prayer meetings, wives groups, Mothers' unions;

meet for study of the Bible or other religious literature;

open libraries or reading rooms;

set up medical centres, sanatoria, nursing homes, hospitals or any kind of welfare programme;

hold jumble sales, bazaars, etc;

produce or distribute religious literature without official permission: this includes even Bibles when they are obtained or printed without state approval.

Ten Worshipping Churches

Edited by Graham Kendrick

'Worship'—the word calls forth images of people flocking to pay honour to God, to show their love and reverence in services as varied as the buildings that enclose them. But what is worship? How can we enliven and enjoy our worship and make it pleasing to God?

Graham Kendrick, well known songwriter and worship leader, draws together ten churches of different affiliations across Britain to discover some surprising and exciting answers to these questions. Gone is the notion of staid, stuffy services. Instead, old frameworks are built upon and polished to a new lustre with experiments in drama, unstructured or free-flowing worship, music, liturgy, and full orchestral accompaniments!

The ten contributors to this book show an understanding for and sensitivity to the feelings of some members of their congregations who wish to maintain tradition, while at the same time an open attitude towards new forms. They write with warmth about what is happening in their churches, charting both the joys and difficulties of worship within a climate of change and sometimes even conflict. What emerges is a dynamic picture of people of varied backgrounds learning to worship together.

A book to encourage and enlighten you!

Published jointly with the British Church Growth Association
192pp   £2.25

Ten New Churches

Edited by Roger Forster

In a nation of redundant churches, what prompts the birth of a new church? An ugent need? An overflowing front room? Enthusiasm for mission and evangelism? Disillusionment with another church?

Ministers and leaders from six denominations across the UK describe the excitement and the setbacks, the people and the growth of their new churches.

Roger Forster, the editor, is pastor of the Ichthus Christian Fellowship in London. Previously he served in the Royal Air Force. The author of *That's a Good Question* and *God's Strategy in Human History*, he brings to this book first-hand experience of planting a new church.

Published jointly with the British Church Growth Association
176pp   £1.95

Ten Sending Churches

Edited by Michael Griffiths

The joy and pain of whole-hearted mission outreach: ten Christian leaders share how they and their churches have caught the vision for mission.

Support for mission is part of most churches' lives, but it is frequently regarded as a boring duty. Here are ten churches, from different areas and traditions, which are taking mission to their hearts. Ideas for raising interest, examples of thoughtful enterprise, imaginative backing for individuals—all are shared, with a wealth of other suggestions. The contributors write with refreshing candour about their failures and successes, offering stimulating insights and innovations.

'A veritable fund of ideas and suggestions … a continual source of reference.' *Church of England Newspaper*

'Worth its weight in gold.' *Today*

Dr Michael Griffiths is Principal of London Bible College and Consulting Director of the Overseas Missionary Fellowship.

Published jointly with STL Books and the Evangelical Missionary Alliance
192pp   £2.25

Ten Growing Churches

Edited by Eddie Gibbs

Here are ten churches, from different areas and denominations, which are seeing their congregations grow and mature.

Eddie Gibbs, who has conducted many Church Growth courses for Bible Society, has chosen ministers from the Anglican, Church of Scotland, Methodist, Baptist, United Reformed, Elim, Free Evangelical and the House Churches. They come from the inner city, suburbia, industrial and rural areas. Together they offer a range of encouraging models, illustrating how God is at work in *ordinary* churches today.

With honesty and courage each has described both successes and failures. There are no check lists or patterns to be slavishly followed—but here is evidence, often dramatic, of God present in power.

Eddie Gibbs is author of several books including *I Believe in Church Growth*. He has recently moved to Pasadena, California, to become Assistant Professor of Church Growth at Fuller Theological Seminary.

Published jointly with the British Church Growth Association
196pp   £1.95

What Is World Vision?

World Vision is a major Christian relief and development agency, founded over 35 years ago. World Vision now helps the hungry, the homeless, the sick and the poor in over 80 countries worldwide.

World Vision is international, interdenominational and has no political affiliation, working wherever possible through local churches and community leaders in close co-operation with the United Nations and other international relief agencies.

Childcare sponsorship is an important part of World Vision's Christian work. Over 400,000 children are currently being cared for in over 2,000 projects.

Sponsors in Europe and around the world are helping thousands of needy children by supplying food, clothing, medical care and schooling. These children usually live with their families although some are in schools or homes. Development and training are usually offered to the communities where the sponsored children live so that whole families can become self-reliant.

World Vision is able to respond with immediate and appropriate relief in crisis situations such as famines, floods, earthquakes and wars. Hundreds of thousands have been saved in Africa through feeding and medical centres. Other projects include cyclone relief for Bangladesh, relief work in Lebanon and medical assistance for medical assistance for Kampuchea.

Over 500 community development projects in 50 countries are helping people to help themselves towards a healthier and more stable future. These projects include agricultural and vocational training, improvements in health care and nutrition (especially for mothers and babies), instruction in hygiene, literacy classes for children and adults, development of clean water supplies and village leadership training.

World Vision's approach to aid is integrated in the sense that we believe in helping every aspect of a person's life and needs. We also help Christian leaders throughout the world to become more effective in their ministry and assist local churches in many lands with their work.

If you would like more information about the work of World Vision, please contact one of the offices listed below:

World Vision of Britain
Dychurch House
8 Abington Street
Northampton
NN1 2AJ, United Kingdom
Tel: 0604 22964

World Vision of Australia
Box 399–C, G P O
Melbourne, 3001 Victoria
Australia
Tel: 613 699 8522

World Vision Deutschland
Postfach 1848
Adenauerallee 32
D–6370 Oberursel
West Germany
Tel: 496171 56074/5/6/7

World Vision International
Christliches Hilfswerk
Mariahilferstr 10/10
A-1070 Wien
Austria
Tel: 0043–222–961 333/366

World Vision International
Christliches Hilfswerk
Badenerstr 87
CH-8004 Zürich
Switzerland
Tel: 0041–1–241 7222

World Vision of Ireland
17 Percy Place
Dublin 4
Eire
Tel: 0001 606 058

Suomen World Vision
Kalevankatu 14 C 13
00100 Helsinki 10
Finland
Tel: 358 90 603422

World Vision of New Zealand
PO Box 1923
Auckland
New Zealand
Tel: 649 770 879

Stichting World
Vision Nederland
Postbus 818
3800 AV Amersfoort
The Netherlands
Tel: 3133 10041

World Vision Canada
6630 Turner Valley Rd
Mississauga, Ontario
Canada L5N 2S4
Tel: 416 821 3030

World Vision International
919 West Huntington Drive
Monrovia
California 91016
United States of America
Tel: 818 303 8811